GHOST HUNTING NORTH CAROLINA

Ghost Hunting North Carolina

First edition 2011
Second edition 2025

Cover and interior design: Hilary Harkness
Editor: Andrew Mollenkof
Proofreader: Jenna Barron
Typesetter: Karla Linder

Front cover mother-daughter photo and interior photos by **Brandon Ambrose** unless otherwise noted.
All photos/illustrations copyright of their respective photographers.
Green background by **RODINA OLENA/shutterstock.com**
Chapter line design by **NATALIA-P/shutterstock:**
ADK branding background by **chyworks/shutterstock.com**

Front cover: **Extezy/shutterstock.com:** design line; **ZillaDigital/shutterstock.com:** diamond pattern; **NATALIA-P/shutterstock:** corner flourishes; **Tirta Sudibya/shutterstock.com:** AHRT antique car; **Zvezdesign/shutterstock.com:** "Ghost Hunting" vector font
Fron and back cover: **Lario Tus/shutterstock.com:** background photo

Cataloging-in-Publication Data on file with the Library of Congress
ISBN 978-1-57860-409-8 (pbk.); 978-1-57860-412-8 (ebook)

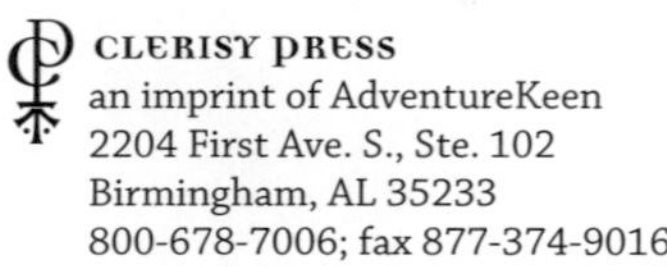
CLERISY PRESS
an imprint of AdventureKeen
2204 First Ave. S., Ste. 102
Birmingham, AL 35233
800-678-7006; fax 877-374-9016

Visit **clerisypress.com** for a complete listing of our books, and for ordering information.

Distributed by Publishers Group West
Printed in China

SAFETY NOTICE: Although Clerisy Press and the author have made every attempt to ensure that the information in this book is accurate at press time, they are not responsible for any loss, damage, injury, or inconvenience that may occur to anyone while using this book. Note that conditions can change from day to day. Minimize your risk on any ghost-hunting expedition by being knowledgeable, prepared, and alert.

KALA AMBROSE

GHOST HUNTING NORTH CAROLINA

YOUR TRAVEL GUIDE TO THE STATE'S MOST HAUNTED PLACES

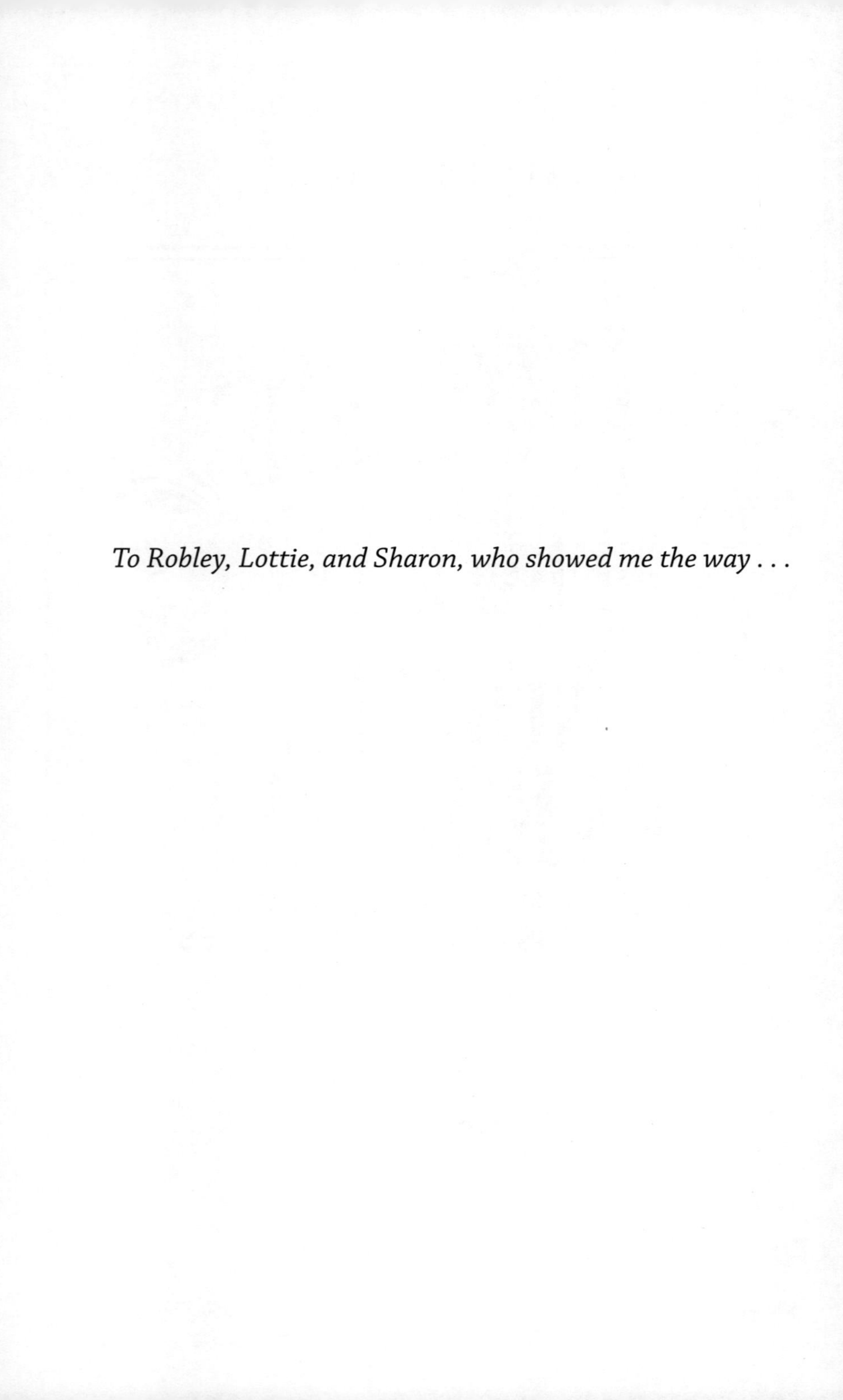

To Robley, Lottie, and Sharon, who showed me the way . . .

TABLE *of* CONTENTS

WELCOME TO AMERICA'S HAUNTED ROAD TRIP

DO YOU BELIEVE IN GHOSTS?

If you are like many Americans, you believe that ghosts walk among us. A CivicScience survey reports that 41% of US adults said they believe in ghosts or spirits, and a solid majority (64%) said they believe in at least one kind of paranormal or supernatural phenomenon. Perhaps you have heard your name called in a dark and empty house. It could be that you have awoken to the sound of footsteps outside your bedroom door, only to find no one there. It is possible that you saw your grandmother sitting in her favorite rocking chair, the same grandmother who had passed away several years before. Maybe you took a photo of a crumbling, deserted farmhouse and discovered strange mists and orbs in the photo, anomalies that were not visible to your naked eye.

If you have experienced similar paranormal events, then you know that ghosts exist. Even if you have not yet experienced these things, you are curious about the paranormal world, the spirit realm. If you weren't, you would not now be reading this preface.

Over the years, I have investigated haunted locations across the country, and with each new site, I found myself becoming more fascinated with ghosts. What are they? How do they manifest themselves? Why are they here? No doubt, you have been asking the same questions.

The books in the America's Haunted Road Trip series can help you find the answers to your questions about ghosts. We've gathered some of America's top ghost writers (no pun intended) and researchers and asked them to write about their states' favorite haunts. Each location that they write about is open to the public so that you can visit them for yourself and try out your ghost-hunting skills. In addition to telling you about their adventures, the writers have included maps and directions so that you can take your own haunted road trip.

People may think that North Carolina is nothing more than beautiful green mountains and miles of sandy beaches, but Kala Ambrose's *Ghost Hunting North Carolina* proves that the mountains are home to shadowy entities that are seen only for an instant before disappearing among the trees, and spirits that leave no footprints in the sands. The book is a spine-tingling trip through the state's various regions with stops at inns, plantations, churches, lighthouses, historic sites, and cemeteries, and even a battleship—all of them haunted. Ride shotgun with Kala as she seeks out Civil War–soldier ghosts at Fort Fisher and the spirits of sailors who served aboard the USS *North Carolina*. Travel with her to Asheville's Grove Park Inn, where the Pink Lady still roams the halls, or sit with her for a spell in the gardens of the Biltmore mansion and watch for the ghostly—and incredibly rich—members of the Vanderbilt family to stroll by. And can that swaggering spirit stalking the moonlit beaches near Beaufort really be the ghost of the infamous pirate Blackbeard? Hang on tight—*Ghost Hunting North Carolina* is a scary ride.

John Kachuba
Editor, America's Haunted Road Trip

INTRODUCTION

Welcome to our journey through *Ghost Hunting North Carolina!*

As your travel guide to the haunted state of North Carolina, it seems appropriate to let you know who is traveling with you on this journey. For as long as I can remember, I've seen ghosts. I was also born psychic, as well as an empath. As a child with these abilities, I didn't quite understand what was happening to me. In large crowds or during the holidays, I would feel the intensity of emotions around me until I would experience severe stomachaches as I absorbed the emotional energy of the people around me.

Later, as I understood what I was experiencing, I learned how not to absorb as much of the energy. I also was able to define the energy that I was feeling, whether it was coming from a person who was upset, or if I was in an area that was holding a significant amount of negative energetic residue. I also learned how to detect if there was a noncorporal entity or spirit around me.

During this time, I also discovered that I had the psychic ability of psychometry, the ability to read the energy imprint that resonates from an object while holding it in your hand or touching it directly. I found that when I put an object in my hand, I could feel its connection to the person who owned it, and sometimes I would see an image of what they had been doing when wearing or using the object.

The first time I became aware of this ability, I was at my grandmother's house and she had let me play with her jewelry. As I went through the jewelry box, I tried on her bracelets, watches, and rings. As I slipped on one of her watches, I had a vivid image of my grandmother with my grandfather when they were much younger. It was like seeing a film clip of them.

I ran to my grandmother and said, "I know what you used to do with Grandpa," and described the scene to her. She asked me who had told me this, and I explained that when I put her watch on my wrist, I saw it. That evening, when my grandfather came home from work, I heard my grandmother ask him if he had told me the story that I had related to her.

To be discreet here, it was a rather romantic story and not one that my grandmother would have been open to sharing in polite company. Hearing the conversation in the other room growing more heated and animated between my grandparents, I ran into the room with the watch and climbed into my grandfather's arms. "Here, Grandpa," I said, "When I put the watch on my arm, it tells me a story." I held the watch on my arm again and began to tell him what I could see. He held his arm around me, gave me a hug, and said that I should take the watch and go put it back in the jewelry box on my grandmother's dressing table. I did as I was told, and as I walked back toward the kitchen where my grandparents were still discussing the event, I heard my grandfather say that I was like him and like his mother, my great-grandmother, who was French and read tea leaves for a living. He said to my grandmother, "She has the gift."

My grandmother never allowed me to play with her jewelry again. Looking back at this now, I have to chuckle. In my innocence at the time, I didn't fully understand the romantic encounter that I saw back then. Now, in my adulthood, I can sympathize with my grandmother and see why having her privacy invaded with that particular memory would be overwhelming. I can also understand, after feeling the intensity and passion of that event, why its memory was imprinted so strongly on the watch. Thus began my understanding of psychometry and my journey of feeling energy in objects.

My first memory of a psychic prediction in childhood was about my little dog. It was bedtime for me, and I became very agitated. I explained to my parents that someone was going to take our dog that night and we needed to bring him inside. My parents tried to calm me down and put me to bed. I slept fitfully all night, sensing the stranger who was going to take our dog. The next morning, as I awoke, I ran outside to find our dog was gone and the gate was thrown wide open. I ran crying to wake up my parents to tell them. My parents have no idea who took the dog, and he was never seen again. With this experience, I began to understand that sometimes I would see or feel psychic events that I would be somewhat powerless to do anything about. This continues at times today when I feel earth changes and weather movements.

Each night before I went to sleep, I would say my prayers, and when I was done, I would often see and sometimes feel an angelic being or a spirit around me. I was raised Catholic and thought it perfectly normal that I would see my guardian angel. I assumed everyone saw spirits and ghosts, and talked with their angel each night before going to sleep.

The first ghost I remember seeing lived right outside my childhood home in Louisiana. In our dining room was a window that looked out to the front yard. My mother had planted orange daylilies out there, and I loved to look at them while sitting at the table in the dining room. One day while I was eating my lunch, I noticed a young boy standing there at the window, looking at me. I smiled and waved at him, and he waved back to me. A moment later he was gone. The next time he appeared,

Kala Ambrose with her mother in front of the window where the young ghost boy would appear.

I noticed something was wrong with part of his head. I called out to my mother to tell her that he was hurt. When she looked through the window, she said no one was there, yet I could still see him standing there. I remember seeing this boy around our home for as long as we lived there. He was very shy and would not speak much. He liked my younger brother and would often appear around him as my brother played outside or in his room. I would always either see him around my brother or standing outside the dining room window in the orange daylilies.

From that point, my experiences continued to grow, from prophetic dreams at night to waking up and realizing that my grandfather was passing away. I experienced his death empathically before anyone else knew it had happened. By the time I was seven, I remember seeing auras, sensing positive and negative energy around people and places, and seeing ghosts and spirits around people, places, and things. I had the good fortune to be raised by parents and grandparents who encouraged my spiritual exploration and education. I was allowed to attend and study almost all forms of religions and their places of worship, and I explored them in depth, beginning in my teen years. My parents also supported my unique abilities. At the age of 13, I began to study tarot and astrology and was creating astrological charts the old-fashioned way (before computers), along with reading tarot for friends. I also began to study the symbols in dreams and dream interpretation, as I have consistently had at least three dreams a night that I can remember. I've classified them into three categories:

teaching and prophetic dreams, which I refer to as "going to night school;" subconscious dreams, which allow us to work through situations here on the earth plane; and dreams with others, where we encounter beings from the spirit world. In my adult years, I began to study many forms of spirituality, including Eastern mysticism, esoteric teachings, earth wisdom, and many others. My connection and interest in the metaphysical, supernatural, and paranormal have only grown over the years, never diminishing.

Along my journey, I came to this understanding: Spirit does not exist in just one location; rather, it is all-encompassing, living within and among us in each moment, thought, and action. I believe that Spirit is raised to its highest level when individuals gather with wisdom, compassion, and a discerning desire to provide service to humanity.

This understanding led me to study and later become a teacher of the ancient wisdom teachings and the hidden mysteries. It also guided me to create the *Explore Your Spirit with Kala* show, where I speak with authors, teachers, researchers, and other experts on metaphysical and paranormal topics.

I've lived in North Carolina for 21 years and have met up with many ghosts who wander this great state. Over the years I've worked to help people here who have experienced problems of a supernatural nature. I am dedicated to the research and exploration of paranormal phenomena in many of its forms, including hauntings, psychic development, and ancient mysteries. I am devoted to compassionate research in these endeavors and present what I believe to be documentation of paranormal activity. This includes, but is not limited to, ghost activity, folklore, exploration of ancient sites and cultures, and other paranormal activity.

What I and others have discovered over the years is that with all of the highly technical equipment available, the best receiver to detect ghosts is still someone with the psychic ability to see or sense the presence of a noncorporal entity.

Since my childhood, I've seen ghosts and restless spirits, and as an adult I've had many experiences with the supernatural and paranormal realms. I've interacted with powerful beings of light, faced encounters with beings from the dark side, and seen ghosts from every walk of life. In my work, I share my experience and training in workshops around the country. I teach others how to become more intuitive, how to connect with the other side, how to sense negative energy in a home or building, and, most important, how to discern whether the energy can be removed and cleansed or whether it is best left alone.

Over the past decade, I have seen a rise in paranormal activity, which corresponds to the lifting of the veil between the earth plane and the spiritual realms at this time. I believe that a conscious evolution is occurring at the mind, body, and spirit level, and as this evolution continues, many people will connect with their intuitive abilities and be able to communicate with the spirit world, including with ghosts who have remained on the earth plane.

I write about some of these experiences on my blog at ExploreYourSpirit.com, and it is now my pleasure to share with you these stories from the ghosts of North Carolina. Each haunted site here has a profound and deeply moving story to tell.

So gather your family and friends, and join me as I share what I see and what I experience as I go ghost hunting across the state of North Carolina. The journey begins in the coastal wetlands of East Carolina, where I explore haunted lighthouses, battleships, and the shipwrecked beaches where Blackbeard and his pirates still roam. Next, I journey across the Piedmont area of North Carolina, where I spend the night in the most actively haunted capitol in the United States and interact with the ghost of a former North Carolina State Governor. My research continues west into the Blue Ridge Mountains, where the ghost known as the Pink Lady and her friends await your presence at the historic Grove Park Inn, where many presidents, celebrities, and ghosts have stayed over the decades.

I visited more than 100 reportedly haunted sites located in North Carolina and culled this list down to the 23 chapters here in this book. My reason for choosing these particular sites had to do first and foremost with finding historical research that confirmed some of the details of the legend of a reportedly haunted site. The second most important criteria in my selection process included being able to confirm reports of ghost activity around the site from a variety of people over a generous span of time. After each site made the cut on these two selections, the final decision then came down to my personal experiences at each of these locations, including what I psychically experienced firsthand at each location relative to paranormal activity. My intent in this book is to provide you with all three of the above-listed criteria in order to assist you in your paranormal research and investigations.

As a psychic and paranormal researcher, I have often been asked what it's like to see or sense a ghost. The best way I can describe the experience is that most of the ghostly activity I immediately feel when entering a new space or building is the time loop/energy imprint type of haunting activity. That's the easiest to detect because it's like seeing a projector playing a movie. To imagine what it looks like to me, picture walking into a home that you have never been in before. You don't know your way around and so you cautiously walk around the house. You have been told that no one is home, but as you continue walking through the rooms, you hear a sound. As your ears strain to detect where the sound is coming from, you hear the soft murmur of voices. You are now fairly sure that someone is here in the home, but you are not sure what room they are in. You're now a little ill at ease because you've been told the house is empty, but you can hear the sound of voices and as you move toward them, they are getting stronger. You see a closed door and can see a bit of light coming from this room, and you softly open the door to see what's inside. As the door opens, you see what looks like an image from a projector that has been left on playing a family movie. The projected image plays a scene from the family's life, and when it ends, it rewinds and plays the movie over and over again. Sometimes the image is crystal clear, and sometimes it's worn and old with parts of the film missing, having burned away like the old celluloid films that would become damaged on the reel in old theaters. Many times, this is similar to what I see, only there's no projector playing, it is just happening in the room, like a 3-D video being projected in the open.

These energy imprints/time loops are the easiest to detect when ghost hunting because they are running on a frequent basis like a movie, appearing nightly at a haunted house near you.

Ghostly visitations and apparitions that I have experienced, on the other hand, are much more subjective, and the ghost has the choice to appear or not appear and decides whether or not to engage with you. This is why on ghost television shows and investigations you will see some investigators attempt to draw out the ghost to interact with them by asking them questions or goading them at times to make them angry enough to show themselves. I don't recommend doing this, as you may run into the wrong ghost who just may decide that rather than hanging around where they have been, they are now angry enough to spend their time hanging around you. One thing ghosts have that we don't is all the time in the world. They don't eat, they don't sleep, and they don't need to work for a living. Would you really want to antagonize a being like this who would have all the time they wanted to mess with you? Or worse, you could find out that it's not a ghost, but an entity that is stronger and could cause even more trouble for you. Most of us don't go to a dangerous part of town and attempt to pick a fight with criminals, inviting someone to show us what they've got, so why would we want to invite this kind of trouble from a ghost? Most of the people I've met who do quickly regret their actions. My advice is to tread lightly and respectfully when ghost hunting. Have respect for the living and the dead at each location, protect yourself at all times, and ask politely to connect with the other side in the same manner you would if you were knocking on a stranger's door and asking to tour their home.

The ghost stories in this book begin in East Carolina. Eastern North Carolina can be lonely and desolate in some places. There are still some areas along the Outer Banks that are only reachable by foot, horseback, or with a 4x4 vehicle. These areas are remote, isolated, and sometimes dangerous.

The shoreline of North Carolina is not welcoming to ships, and even with the abundance of lighthouses warning ships to steer clear, the number of shipwrecks reported along the coast is in the hundreds. Pirate ghosts wander the land, looking to save their sunken ships, hide their treasure, or settle a score. Blackbeard is the most famous and infamous of them all, and remains in good company with the men and women who followed a similar path.

Traveling along the coastline and the Outer Banks, I visited areas where nature looks untouched. The land appears as fresh as the day early European settlers arrived to colonize the area, including young Virginia Dare and the legend of the Lost Colony of Roanoke. Standing there looking at the shore, I was touched by the beauty of the land and sea and by the bravery of those early colonists who arrived here not knowing what was in store for them. I'm struck by the fact that here on these tiny barrier islands, we now have 24-hour communications advising us of hurricanes days before the storms arrive in order to evacuate to safety. In the days of the early colonists, there was little warning, and the wind and waves crashing down on these tiny islands had to be extremely frightening to both the living and the dead.

Join me as we step back into time and walk in the footsteps of pirates, colonists, adventurers, plantation owners, and the people who loved them. Perhaps Blackbeard will finally share where his treasure has been buried all this time.

Some believe that your soul can't rest when you are lost at sea, and thus you remain a ghost. The coast of North Carolina is full of stories of ghosts said to appear and disappear at will, some to warn of approaching storms, others on patrol to guard a fort, and lighthouse keepers who remain at their station long after their final retirement.

I find it interesting to note that should you sail directly east from the coast of North Carolina, you will reach Bermuda, putting you directly into the Bermuda Triangle. Were the souls who dared to cross the Bermuda Triangle to enter the North Carolina coast doomed even before they began?

As with all of the America's Haunted Road Trip books, travel information is provided for each haunted location for those brave enough to make the journey in person to see these sites for themselves and for paranormal researchers who are interested in exploring haunted North Carolina.

Tuck *Ghost Hunting North Carolina* in your pocket and take the journey behind the scenes with detailed historic and personal information that I share about each destination. Happy haunting!

All the best,
Kala Ambrose

The Old Settler's Cemetery in Charlotte has a park-like setting.
(See Chapter 23, page 201)

Roanoke
Tarboro
Creswell
New Bern
Cape Hatteras
Beaufort
Atlantic Beach
Wilmington
Kure Beach

EAST CAROLINA

THE COAST AND OUTER BANKS

The Bellamy Mansion is an example of antebellum architecture in North Carolina.

CHAPTER 1

WILMINGTON

THE SPIRITED REVIVAL OF BELLAMY MANSION

Dr. John Bellamy was a man of fortitude, and the mansion he built is a spectacular example of North Carolina architecture. Located in downtown Wilmington, the 22-room mansion is a stunning example of Greek Revival style. The mansion gives the impression of being a most inviting place; the formal gardens draw you in with their delightful colors and scents, and the towering columns give the sense of strength and stability. It's easy to imagine a carefree life spent here by Dr. Bellamy, his wife, Eliza, and their 10 children. Dr. Bellamy was a prominent and highly regarded physician and businessman in the area. Along with his medical practice, he owned a turpentine distillery, served as a director of the Cape Fear Bank, and was a stockholder of the Wilmington Railroad. While walking through each room, images of tea parties, elaborate dinners, and mint juleps on the veranda come to mind.

The Bellamy family moved into their new home in March 1861. The life of Dr. Bellamy and his family was not without strife, though. Two months after the family moved in, the state of North Carolina seceded from the Union to enter the Civil War on the side of the Confederacy.

Dr. Bellamy was the owner of several plantations, and his slaves had been forced to do some of the construction of the Bellamy Mansion. One of the most well-known slaves was William Gould, who escaped from the mansion's slave quarters in a rowboat, which he navigated down the Cape Fear River until he encountered a Union ship. His diary reports that he boarded the ship and immediately joined the Union Navy.

As the war began, the Bellamy family continued to reside in their home until an epidemic of yellow fever struck the area. The disease, coupled with nearby Fort Fisher falling to Union troops, led the family to retreat to their country home, Grovely Plantation.

The Union army captured Wilmington, and General Joseph Hawley claimed the Bellamy Mansion as his headquarters and home. He refused to allow Dr. Bellamy to enter the mansion and went so far as to deny him entrance to the city of Wilmington. The Union government seized control of southern land, business property, and homes during this time, and it took years for Dr. Bellamy to recover his home. Almost four years later, in 1865, Dr. Bellamy traveled to Washington, D.C., to receive a presidential pardon in order to have his home returned to him.

After the war, the family began to restore the home. Mrs. Bellamy decided to build a black wrought iron fence around the house so she could create a formal garden. This garden is still lovingly tended to this day and can be enjoyed on the tour along with the rest of the mansion.

The black wrought iron fence caught my attention. There are supernatural teachings that state that wrought iron is reputed to hold spirits inside the area where the fence is built. Ghosts need energy to manifest, and iron, as a conductor of electricity, will ground the ghost when it comes into contact with the iron. Wrought iron fences around cemeteries were used in this capacity: They worked as a barrier to keep unwanted spirits beyond the fence and also to contain spirits that reside inside the fenced area. Iron horseshoes were also hung above front doors in the old days, as they were said to bring good luck by keeping a house free from unwanted spirits.

Unknowingly, when Mrs. Bellamy had the wrought iron fence constructed around the mansion, she may have created a barrier that holds ghosts inside the Bellamy Mansion today.

The Bellamy children grew up to be successful in their own rights, including John Jr., who became a US congressman. I found it intriguing, though, that out of the four daughters, only one married (Belle). One of the girls, Kate, died in infancy. The other two daughters, Eliza and Ellen, lived out the remainder of their lives together in the Bellamy Mansion. Eliza passed away in 1927, and Ellen died in 1946.

The house stood quiet until 1972, when the nonprofit Bellamy Mansion Corporation began restoration of the home in order to preserve the mansion. A few weeks after restoration began, a fire broke out in the home, destroying a large portion of the interior. The house was stabilized after the fire, and interior restoration resumed in 1992.

In 1994, the fully restored Bellamy Mansion opened as a museum offering tours of the house and gardens. As I visited the Bellamy Mansion, I kept myself open to receiving any energetic disturbances inside the home and was on the lookout for ghostly activity. The northeast corner of the land is where the original slave quarters were located, and it can't help but be a somber area. Beyond this section, what I felt most around Bellamy Mansion was peaceful and restful. I felt a strong feminine presence in several parts of the mansion. While a spirit did not appear during my time at Bellamy Mansion, I could feel her energy. My feeling was that it was one of the sisters who lived most of her life in the home and simply never left.

Local stories suggest that daughter Ellen, who passed in 1946, still haunts the home. There are reports of hearing her wheelchair moving around various parts of the home. People have reported seeing a woman in a ball gown near the front door and on the front porch. Smudged handprints have also appeared overnight on the wall in Ellen's bedroom and been found by staff the next day.

A woman in an elegant ball gown has been seen near the front door and porch area by a wide variety of local witnesses and visitors to the home. Many believe it to be the ghost of Ellen, the daughter who never married and the last of the original family to live in Bellamy Mansion.

There are also a few reports of a Union soldier seen walking through the home, but most likely, this is an energy imprint, which is a time loop of captured energy that replays itself on a frequent basis. With an energetic imprint haunting, the ghost does not interact with the living, nor are they aware of the current time. The energy imprint just plays and replays the action, which was charged with the emotional intensity of such a strong nature that it has left behind an energetic recording.

Bellamy Mansion may be haunted, but the energy of the mansion is warm and welcoming, and Miss Ellen seems to enjoy opening her home to guests. The Bellamy Mansion hosts weddings and other special events throughout the year, and the caretakers of the home, both living and in spirit, appear to be pleased with the results.

CHAPTER 2

WILMINGTON

THE HAUNTING OF THE USS *NORTH CAROLINA* BATTLESHIP

The USS *North Carolina*, commissioned in 1941, was considered one of the greatest weapons on the sea.

Commissioned in 1941, the vessel USS *North Carolina* was considered to be one of the world's most formidable ships. During World War II, the *North Carolina* participated in every major naval offensive in the Pacific, earning 15 battle stars, and was known as the protector of aircraft carriers—it even saved the USS *Enterprise* in 1942.

On December 7, 1941, the Japanese bombed Pearl Harbor using 353 fighters, dive bombers, and torpedo planes. Four battleships were sunk, and four others damaged. Two destroyers and three cruisers were sunk, and almost 350 aircraft were destroyed or severely damaged. More than 2,300 men were killed, and more than 1,100 were injured. The overwhelming devastation was a huge shock to the nation.

After the attack on Pearl Harbor, much of the Pacific Fleet was destroyed. The first-wave Japanese attack inflicted most of the damage, and the second wave returned to demolish anything left standing. Japan and the United States were in peace talks at the time, so the attack came as a surprise. No declaration of war had been delivered before the attack. After this act, the United States declared war and entered World War II.

The surviving sailors in Hawaii had lost many of their friends, along with many vessels, and they no doubt felt isolated on an island far away from the mainland. The attack had been swift.

Then one day, the first major naval ship arrived in Hawaii. It was the USS *North Carolina,* and she was greeted with mass celebration by an overwhelming crowd of soldiers, sailors, marines, and Air Force pilots hailing her presence from the beaches with cheers and delight. Upon her arrival in Hawaii, many sailors were quoted as saying that she was "the most beautiful thing they had ever seen."

In my experience as a psychic and paranormal investigator, I have found that powerful emotional experiences of the most positive and the most negative nature leave an energy imprint on the object of the attention. Energy imprints are also left on objects surrounding the area. I believe that the USS *North Carolina* battleship soaked up all of that energy that day upon her arrival in Pearl Harbor. In the water and in the air, she felt the pain and loss from the destruction that had occurred, while at the same time, she was greeted and filled with joy by sailors, pilots, and marines who saw her as a saving grace and point of hope. This, I believe, buoyed the battleship, giving her great luck and fierce determination in battle.

She was known to be a feisty fighter; stories are still told about the day she fought her first battle against the Japanese Imperial Navy. Her guns roared and surrounded her in so much smoke that the nearby USS *Enterprise* reported that they believed her to be on fire. When the smoke cleared, the facts showed just the opposite. The great lady had shot down seven planes and reportedly assisted in bringing down seven more, and she was just getting started. She also fought in Okinawa, where amid a fierce battle, she shot down her share of Japanese kamikaze pilots.

During the war, the Japanese reported on their radio six different times that they had sunk the *North Carolina* battleship, all of which proved to be false. The Japanese did manage to hit the ship once with a torpedo, which cost five crewmen their lives. Five other men died aboard the ship from other circumstances, and by some accounts, some of them still remain on board and on active duty on the ship to this day.

The USS *North Carolina* battleship is now anchored in Wilmington, North Carolina, where thousands visit her each year. Many of those who visit and work on the ship have shared a number of ghost stories and other paranormal activity they experienced while on board.

From the night watchman who sleeps aboard the ship each night to daily tourists and visitors, the reports of the ship being haunted continue to grow. Some of the ghosts are harmless, though they do catch people off guard, giving them a fright. Mostly, they are seen involved in their daily activities aboard the ship, looking for lunch from the kitchen, preparing for bed in their bunks, and performing maintenance around the ship. The sounds of their banging as they work on parts of the ship can often be heard throughout the night. These ghosts are hard workers; they bang with their tools, knock on walls, open and close hatches, yell at each other, have heated and animated discussions, and enjoy turning televisions and lights on and off.

The ship is massive, and as you approach where she's anchored on the Cape Fear River, you can't help but feel excited and swell with a sense of patriotic pride. Upon boarding the ship, you take a step back into history. As you walk through each section, displays are set up to show what life on the ship was like. Life-size cardboard cutouts of men are arranged in some of the rooms, such as the barbershop, movie theater, post office, laundry room, ice-cream shop, and infirmary. It quickly sinks in that each ship was a world of its own, where sailors lived for months at sea in cramped conditions, and where all of their daily needs had to be met.

The battleship offers a Ghost Ship weekend when you can explore the ship with tour guides to see the most haunted areas. I was fortunate on the day I visited that it was a quiet day, midweek, and I was allowed to wander through the ship at my own pace. This allowed me to take my time and linger in some places where I felt the energy shift around me. What I felt first and foremost was a strong emotional bond linked here on the ship. The men who had served on this ship were extremely proud of their work and their commitment to their country. You can literally feel this pride in the air.

When World War II ended, the ship was sent to inactive reserve in 1947 in New Jersey. In 1958, it was announced that the ship would be sent to the scrap heap to be torn apart and the metal recycled. Citizens of North Carolina formed a group called SOS (Save Our Ship) and raised the money to purchase the ship and bring it home to Wilmington.

In 1962, the USS *North Carolina* was delivered to the state of North Carolina and dedicated as a memorial to all World War II veterans and those who died in the war.

Five sailors died aboard the USS *North Carolina* when a Japanese torpedo hit the ship's hull in 1942. Five other men have died aboard the ship due to other circumstances. The ghosts appear in many parts of the ship, including the kitchen area.

As I took in the emotional energy resonating from the ship, I compared it to other naval ships I have been on, and I found the *North Carolina* to be quite different in feeling. I've been on several naval ships, including going on a Tiger cruise, where family and friends are invited to cruise on a naval ship as it returns from a deployment, so I'm familiar with the look and feel of a ship. I've stepped through my share of bulkheads to enter rooms, and I appreciate the tremendous amount of thought and planning that goes into building a ship to house so many sailors in one confined space.

As I walked through the ship, I noticed that there were certainly pockets that felt sad (the brig area being a strong one) and a couple of areas that felt very creepy, but overall, the ship bursts with pride. It rings from the walls, and I think the veterans and tourists who visit the ship each day reinforce this energy, building it to even greater levels.

For the most part, according to history, the men on the ship got along very well and were as happy as they could be when involved in wartime activity. But there was one man aboard that ship who appears as if he has never been happy, and he continues to haunt the ship until this day. I felt his presence on the ship after only being there for a few minutes. If he was a sailor on the *North Carolina* during the war, I feel that he caused trouble and mayhem aboard the ship as often as he could. I encountered him during my visit to the *North Carolina,* and I'm not sure that he is a ghost. I think instead that he may be a malevolent spirit that has attached itself to the ship.

At one point during my tour, I sensed the presence of another ghost, and I began to track it around the ship. I encountered stepping into cold spots, following the sound of footsteps where no one was walking, and overhearing a bit of conversation near the mess hall. I became a psychic detective, using my internal radar to guide me to the energy as it would grow and then disappear. Near the ship's galley, I saw a shadowy mist begin to appear. I quickly reached for my camera to snap a picture.

Before I could take the photo, the entire camera shut down, and the brand-new batteries that I had loaded that morning were completely drained. I always travel with extra batteries; as any paranormal researcher can tell you, that is a frequent occurrence when ghosts are near that the batteries in all types of electronic equipment will be drained. This ghost that had appeared, though, was not the dark presence I had felt earlier on the ship, as he did not emit the intense feeling of dread that I had detected earlier with the malevolent spirit. He appeared to be involved in his daily activities and seemed more interested in getting lunch from the galley area than anything else.

The ship itself makes it difficult to take photos that could realistically be used as evidence of paranormal activity. Besides the fact that the ship is mostly metal and the flash from the camera bounces everywhere, many of the displays on the ship are behind glass, which also makes it difficult to take pictures without light of some kind bouncing off the glass and metal and creating the effect of orbs and other anomalies that could be misconstrued as supernatural in nature. I loaded new batteries in my camera but decided that it was time to put the gadgets away and use the best tool I have—my psychic sense. I continued through the ship for about a half hour after that, no longer sensing the ghostly presence. The ship has been wonderfully restored, and it was a pleasure just to take the self-guided tour of this living legend.

Just as I was about to wrap things up and head for the exit, the angry spirit appeared. I was standing by some stairs when I noticed someone looking at me.

The only way I know to describe him to you is that he was intense, forbidding, and not at all interested in conversation. Reports from various paranormal investigators and researchers have said that the man they encountered offered his name and, at times, his rank. The being that I encountered was not in the mood to talk, and though he startled me at first, I soon realized that he wasn't particularly interested in me at that moment, unless he thought I would be interfering with his activities. He was not the ghost I had seen materializing near the mess hall; that presence had been fun to follow around the ship. He was pleasant enough and simply engaged in his daily activities. This entity, on the other hand, sucked the energy out of the area where he appeared and filled it with angry energy. I held my ground, using what I had been taught over the years to keep a protective shield of light energy around me so as not to allow him to come any closer to me.

The entire encounter lasted a few seconds and felt like several minutes. I know nothing about this spirit, not his name nor his rank, but I do know what I felt when meeting him. He's moved past the point of being reasonable; anger has overtaken him, and it's how he feeds his energy. He takes the form of a man when he appears, but I don't think that his true form is human. I feel that this spirit attached itself to one of the men who served on the ship and now uses that man's form to manifest as a human when it desires. The sailor to whom he attached himself during the time he served on the ship was never a mentally well-balanced person. He wrestled with his dark side all throughout his life and enjoyed being cruel to others onboard, which made him prey for this dark spirit.

He's definitely not giving out information as to whether or not he was one of the men who died aboard the ship, but it's clear that he's attached to the ship with no plans to leave anytime soon. Should you encounter him during your visit, you'll know immediately. Even if you do not see him, you'll feel his presence, a mixture of anger and dread, and you'll struggle not to run as far away from this energy as you can.

As I kept my light force field shield around me, the spirit disappeared and I could no longer detect his presence. He's motivated by creating fear and making other people feel afraid, so if you bump into him on the ship, don't engage with him. The best thing you can do if you run into him is to ignore him and move away to another area.

If you encounter the other ghosts here on the ship, they feel very different from this spirit. Should they materialize in front of you, they are lighter in color and go about their daily tasks on the ship. In comparison, the dark spirit appears to be hunting for something or someone on the ship.

Finished with the tour, I gathered myself and prepared to disembark. Turning back to look at the ship one last time, I found myself agreeing with those sailors in Hawaii; the ship is a beautiful sight. Wonderfully preserved, we can't quite call her a landmark, but she is a presence to be dealt with and honored. The nickname given to the USS *North Carolina* was The Showboat, and she continues to live up to her name today.

THE LIFE AND LEGEND OF BLACKBEARD'S GHOST

Blackbeard the Pirate may be the most famous pirate ever known, and his legend, his legacy, and his ghost remain with us to this day. His proper name was Edward Teach. He gained the nickname of Blackbeard from his long mass of tousled black hair that whipped around his head, as well as his scruffy black beard. They gave him a dark, forbidding look, and it was reported at times that he would place lit fuses under his hat that would shower his face with sparks, in order to further intimidate and scare people.

He was ruthless as a pirate, but reports also state that no captive of his was ever injured or killed. Before his death in 1718, Blackbeard lived in several areas of North Carolina, including the villages of Bath and Beaufort. Blackbeard's final battle was with Lieutenant Maynard of the British Navy on Ocracoke Island. Blackbeard fought valiantly with his sword but in the end was overtaken by the sheer numbers of Maynard's crew. By the time he was taken down, he had been shot five times and stabbed more than 20 times.

Once he was confirmed dead, Lieutenant Maynard ordered that Blackbeard's head be cut off and hung from the bow of Maynard's ship. Blackbeard's headless body was then thrown into the water near Ocracoke Island.

Reports of Blackbeard's ghost began in the 1800s. Locals reported seeing and hearing an epic battle with ghostly ships and men waging war against each other near Bath Creek and the inlet. Massive balls of fire were also seen moving back and forth across the water toward the ships. Legends state that Blackbeard's ghost most often appears right before a storm rages along the coast of Ocracoke, Bath, Albemarle, and Pamlico Sound. He seems drawn to the sea when the waves pick

THE LIFE AND LEGEND OF BLACKBEARD'S GHOST (CONTINUED)

up and are thrashing, and some say he is looking for his head. There is often a light seen accompanying his ghost, which is referred to as Teach's Light.

Blackbeard continues to roam the coast of North Carolina and is said to frequently visit the coastal towns where he once lived. On a dark stormy night, don't be surprised if you run into the pirate walking along the coast.

CHAPTER 3

KURE BEACH

CIVIL WAR GHOSTS OF FORT FISHER

Fort Fisher was one of the largest forts built of earth and sand. In 1865, it covered 1 mile of sea defense and ⅓ of a mile of land defense.

Fort Fisher is located near the Cape Fear River and is one of the largest forts built in the South. The entrance to the fort is imposing, and the giant oaks surrounding the fort stand as guardians with deep, sorrowful stories to tell. The construction of the fort is interesting; rather than being built of brick and mortar, it was made with earth and sand in order to absorb the shock waves from explosions.

The fort's ramparts were built to be 32 feet high and were connected by underground passages and a telegraph system. More than 1,000 men worked to complete the fort, and upon its completion, 22 guns faced the ocean, and another 25 guns covered the approach by land.

In 1864, Wilmington was the last major seaport to remain open during the Civil War to receive goods smuggled in from blockade-runners, the others having been blockaded or occupied by Federal forces. Norfolk, Virginia, fell in May of 1862, and the supply line in Wilmington was the last one standing to deliver necessities to Robert E. Lee's men in Virginia and other troops further inland. The only reason that the port of Wilmington was still open was due to the protection provided by Fort Fisher.

On Christmas Eve 1864, Union troops and ships attacked Fort Fisher and bombarded the fort through Christmas Day. The troops then retreated after two unsuccessful days of fighting. Union forces returned in January of 1865 when they bombed the fort from tactical areas both on land and by sea for almost three days. At the end of these three days, more than 9,000 Union soldiers attacked the fort. With these large numbers, they were able to take the fort by nightfall.

When Fort Fisher fell to Union troops, it was one of the final nails in the coffin of the Confederate army. They evacuated the area, and the port of Wilmington was no longer able to receive smuggled goods. With supplies cut off, the Civil War ended soon after.

After the battle was over, Union troops occupied Fort Fisher, using it to hold Confederate prisoners and to serve as a base of operations. On January 16, 1865, the fort's main magazine mysteriously exploded, killing more than 200 Union soldiers and Confederate prisoners. Shortly after this time, ghost stories began to be reported.

One of the ghosts reported to haunt Fort Fisher is the Confederate spy Rose O'Neal Greenhow, also known as Rebel

Rose. Rose was considered to be one of the most important female spies of the Civil War. Born in Maryland, Rose's family were slave owners, and she grew up a socialite in Washington, D.C. Among her close friends were John Calhoun, James Buchanan, and Dolley Madison. Rose married Robert Greenhow, and they traveled to San Francisco during the gold rush, where Robert died in a tragic accident. Rose returned to Washington and was known for her social skills and her love affairs with prominent men. This led to the large amount of information she received regarding Union plans for the Civil War.

Rose Greenhow (Rebel Rose) and her daughter (Little Rose) while imprisoned at the Old Capitol Prison in Washington, D.C., in 1862. *(Photo courtesy of WikiCommons)*

One of her greatest accomplishments as a spy was delivering a coded message to General Beauregard that enabled him to win the First Battle of Bull Run. She was eventually captured and imprisoned, along with her 8-year-old daughter. This backfired for the Union as a public relations campaign, as Rose became a martyr for the Confederate cause. Even while imprisoned she managed to continue to run a spy ring, sneaking out messages in secret places, including tying the messages inside the buns of other women's hair.

In 1862, she stood trial for espionage and gave a passionate speech in which she asked the court questions such as this: "If Mr. Lincoln's friends pass along such important information to her on such a frequent basis, shouldn't they be looked into as well for espionage?" The Union judge, knowing that she was already being covered heavily in the press for her imprisonment with her young daughter, decided it would be best to release her with the decree that she must return to the South and never return to the North again. When she was released, she exited the prison draped in a Confederate flag.

At that point, she traveled to Europe to campaign for assistance to the Confederacy as a diplomatic emissary of Jefferson Davis. It was during this time that she wrote her book, *My Imprisonment and the First Year of Abolition Rule at Washington,* which was a bestseller. She also met with Queen Victoria and Napoleon III during her time in Europe.

During her return from Europe, Rose was aboard a blockade runner that ran aground off the coast of North Carolina near Fort Fisher during a fierce storm. The legend states that Rose asked to be placed in a rowboat so she could leave the ship and reach the shore before nearby Union ships captured the damaged blockade runner boat.

The rowboat carrying Rose overturned in the strong waves, and Rose drowned. She was reportedly carrying several thousand dollars worth of gold from the proceeds she earned by selling her book in Europe. The gold was sewn into her clothing, and the weight of it pulled her under in the stormy seas. It was also reported that she was carrying several bags with secret messages from Europe that would have benefitted the Confederate Army.

Legend states that a soldier found her body washed up on shore and that he stole the gold from the bags sewn to her clothing. Rose was buried in Oakdale Cemetery in Wilmington, North Carolina. The legend also reports that the man who stole the gold from Rebel Rose's body felt so guilty that he later returned the money to her estate.

Rose's ghost is most often reported not at the cemetery but rather near the shore heading toward Fort Fisher. It appears that she is still trying to complete her mission and deliver the messages from Europe to the Confederate army.

During my time at Fort Fisher, I checked out the fiber-optic battle map, which uses sound effects and flashing lights to give a sense of what the battle felt like during this time. The flashes portray the charged energy experienced by Union and Confederate soldiers during this siege. While this portrayal brings home how intensely the fort was attacked, I found the most eerie time to be when walking alone around the fort. Certain areas were so still and empty. Yet, as I walked further around the various sections of the fort, there were old sounds that began to rise from the building, including whispers coming from around corners, the sound of shuffling feet perhaps from imprisoned soldiers, and the sound of heavy boots pacing back and forth from a soldier on guard duty.

Fort Fisher was called back into action during World War II, when it was used as a training site for anti-aircraft artillerymen. As the war raged on, German U-boats were reported off the coast of North Carolina and were responsible for sinking several American ships. There is also a legend that German sailors from a submarine were caught near Fort Fisher on their way to plant dynamite and blow up the channel that allowed naval ships to move throughout the area near the port of Wilmington. The rough and ready battle feeling in this area still permeates the land. Many ghost sightings are reported of soldiers pacing around the fort at night, and shots are heard in the distance.

During my tour of the fort in broad daylight, I was surrounded by tourists and families exploring the area. Even with so many living people around, I could feel the ghosts of both Union and Confederate soldiers who never left the battle. I wanted to stay overnight at Fort Fisher, but that is not permitted. Should anyone be left there alone on a moonlit night, I believe that the ghosts of Fort Fisher would certainly pay a visit to anyone trespassing in their fort.

THE GHOSTS OF CURRITUCK BEACH LIGHTHOUSE

The North Carolina coast is one of the most dangerous of the Atlantic for ships. The unpredictable and treacherous currents and ever-shifting sandbars have run more ships aground here than anywhere else along the Eastern Seaboard, giving the North Carolina coast the nickname Graveyard of the Atlantic. This is why so many lighthouses were built in the state, as a warning to sailors as they approached the coastline.

Built in 1875, the Currituck Beach Lighthouse is located to the north of Bodie Island and was the last major lighthouse built on the Outer Banks. Its most distinguishing feature may be that it remains in its original brick form, rather than being painted in a bold black-and-white pattern like most other North Carolina lighthouses.

Each lighthouse hired what was called a "keeper," a man who would care for the lighthouse and ensure that the light was in good working order at all times. A small cottage was built next to each lighthouse in order to house the keeper and his family. Once construction was complete on the lighthouse and cottage, the first lighthouse keeper for the Currituck Beach Lighthouse settled into the cottage with his wife and their daughter, Sadie. Sadie slept in what is referred to as the north bedroom of the cottage.

One day, Sadie was playing on the beach and went missing. Her body was found washed up on shore the next day. Shortly after her demise, reports of the ghost of a little girl began to appear around the lighthouse and the cottage. Rumors began to spread that the keeper's cottage was cursed and that illness, misery, and death fell to anyone who slept in the north bedroom. Over the years, lighthouse keepers and their guests who slept in the north bedroom reported seeing and feeling a ghost in the room, and several became ill while staying in the room.

Ghostly apparitions and other restless spirits are frequently seen and reported around the lighthouse. Until recently, it was unclear why so many spirits appeared in this area. In 2009, after a ferocious winter storm along the Outer Banks, waves from the Atlantic Ocean dredged up a shipwreck, placing it at the edge of the shore. The ship appears to be from the early 1600s and may be the oldest shipwreck ever found along the coast of North Carolina. East Carolina University (ECU) students, underwater archaeologists, maritime history experts, and members from the North Carolina Wildlife Resources Commission worked around the clock in a race against the tide to pull the shipwreck farther up the beach to safety. The ECU team continues to work on identifying the ship; most recently, coins were found with fleur-de-lis symbols on one side and the image of King Louis XIII on the other. While the name of the ship, along with her crew and passengers, has not yet been identified, such a large ship most likely was carrying a full load of goods and passengers.

The ship sank more than 200 years before the Currituck Beach Lighthouse was built near its underwater grave. It's very likely that the ghostly passengers wandered the coast of Currituck Beach for hundreds of years and now make the Currituck Lighthouse and keeper's cottage their home. Many also suspect that young Sadie may have been lured into the ocean after seeing one of the ghosts in the water, which led to her drowning.

Built in 1843, Fort Macon was one of several coastal forts built to protect the entrance to North Carolina ports, including Beaufort and Morehead City.

CHAPTER 4

ATLANTIC BEACH

THE HAUNTED SOLDIERS OF FORT MACON

The War of 1812 prompted the United States to build a long line of forts along the East Coast for national security. Built by the U.S. Army Corp of Engineers, Fort Macon was designed to protect Beaufort Harbor, a deepwater ocean port. The fort is five sided, built of brick and stone, is quite striking. Twenty-six vaulted rooms called casements make up the substantial fort, with walls that are almost five feet thick.

The fort became active in 1834, and at the beginning of the Civil War the Confederacy of North Carolina wrestled the port away from Union soldiers. The fort was recovered by Union soldiers in 1862 and served as a federal prison for both civil and military prisoners from 1867 to 1876. Fort Macon was officially closed in 1903. The state of North Carolina purchased the fort from the federal government in 1923 and turned it into a state park. It was reactivated for a brief period during World War II as a coastal defense base.

Visually appealing, the fort and surrounding park lie on one of North Carolina's most beautiful barrier islands. The park is fully restored and open to the public. Besides the fort, there are areas for fishing and swimming, nature trails to hike, a refreshment stand, and beautiful scenery on land and sea to enjoy, which makes the fort and the park one of the most visited parks in the state, reportedly receiving more than 1 million visitors each year.

In 1862, Union forces attacked the fort, and even though the Confederate soldiers were completely surrounded, they refused to surrender. The fort was besieged by heavy gunfire for 11 hours straight, and cannon fire struck the fort more than 500 times. By the next day, the fort was under such strain that the commander, Colonel White, was forced to surrender. While the fort had been able to easily withstand gunfire, cannons quickly penetrated the barriers.

Some reports state that Civil War ghosts haunt the fort, including Confederate soldiers who keep watch for approaching Union soldiers. Others state that the ghosts there are those of former prisoners. Witnesses report seeing soldiers strolling outside the fort and seeing items move within several rooms inside the fort. There are also sounds of footsteps, gunfire, and men speaking in low voices.

Ghosts of Civil War soldiers are reported to still be on active duty, guarding the fort day and night.

The fort is beautiful in its own way, and the five-sided shape is intriguing. Exhibits and displays include the fort's powder magazines, counterfire rooms with cannons, and furnace and bake ovens. Some quarters have been restored to show how soldiers and officers lived at the fort.

While touring Fort Macon, I didn't experience any paranormal activity. It was a gorgeous day when we visited the area, and everyone there was enjoying the beautiful weather. Some of the techniques used in ghost hunting include checking for increased solar activity, which has been reported by many paranormal researchers to cause an increase in paranormal activity, as spirits need an energy source in order to appear. When the sun has a solar storm or is releasing solar flares, radioactive particles enter the Earth's atmosphere, which charges the geomagnetic fields. Ghosts can then access this energy, which allows them to be more active on the earth plane. Moon phases have also been studied, and certain phases, including the full moon cycle, often produce more ghost sightings and paranormal activity.

During my visit, the geomagnetic field was quiet, and solar storms were low. I was also there during a low lunar cycle. I didn't detect any paranormal activity to note other than the usual energy imprints I detect any time I'm near a battlefield. This doesn't mean that the fort is not haunted; it just means that I didn't encounter any activity during my visit. As with any paranormal investigation, it often takes time and repeated visits to a location under the right conditions to find proof of ghostly activity. Locals and visitors continue to report ghostly experiences while visiting.

THE FLAMING SHIP OF NEW BERN

In New Bern, North Carolina, the Atlantic Ocean meets the Neuse River, providing an idyllic setting to spend a vacation on the beach each summer under sunny and star-filled skies. Gentle, warm breezes drift in from the ocean, and many locals and tourists enjoy a peaceful stroll on the beach under the moonlight. Yet on one night of the year, a horrifying site appears on the water near New Bern.

In the early 1700s, a group of German Protestants hired a captain and crew to sail them from England to North Carolina. Their plans were to settle in New Bern and begin their new lives there. Groups of Germans, like these, were often referred to as Palatines. They carried all their worldly goods with them, and reportedly they had quite a large amount of gold and silver, which they had kept hidden from the captain and crew.

As the ship approached the North Carolina coast, the Palatines excitedly prepared for the landing, pulling their belongings up onto the deck. They were preparing to disembark from the ship as quickly as possible. The captain and crew, seeing the substantial wealth of the Palatines, told them that for their own safety, the landing could not be made until the next morning.

That evening, as the Palatine passengers slept aboard the ship, the crew stabbed and killed all of them. They collected all of the Palatines' gold and silver and loaded it into rowboats. As the captain and crew made their escape, they set fire to the ship to destroy any evidence of the Palatine passengers. The ship quickly caught fire, and as the murderous captain and crew watched, the ship became engulfed in flames, but to their surprise, it never sank. Instead, while on fire, it began to sail toward them. Terrified, the crew rowed as quickly as

possible to shore and ran to hide in the woods. Local reports at the time stated that at daybreak the ship was no longer on fire, but it still remained floating on the water in a blackened and charred state. That evening, the ship appeared to be on fire again, and then sailed away out to sea until it disappeared from the horizon.

Each year, during the first night of the new moon in September, the "Flaming Ship of New Bern"—as described by locals—is reported to make its appearance off the shores of New Bern. Others say that it now appears during the full moon of a summer evening in July or August, and other reports say that it is during the first full moon in September.

It has also been reported as the "Flaming Ship of Ocracoke." The legend states that the Palatines were supposed to live in New Bern but that they were killed on the ship near Ocracoke. Witnesses have reported seeing the ship in both locations. Perhaps the Palatines are chasing the evil captain and crew along the entire watery trail. The oldest reports date back to seeing the ship off the coast of Ocracoke, while more recent sightings report the ship near New Bern. Over the years, it looks as if the Palatines are drawing ever closer to the place they wanted to call home.

The ship reportedly appears out of nowhere and burns brightly in the water three times before disappearing as quickly as it appeared. Local lore states that the Palatines will appear each year in search of their treasure. Until they have their gold and silver returned to them, they refuse to rest in peace and are looking for revenge on the captain and his crew.

What happened to Virginia Dare and the rest of the colonists of Roanoke remains a mystery to this day.

CHAPTER 5

ROANOKE

THE LOST COLONY OF ROANOKE

In 1584, explorers were sent to Roanoke Island (a narrow island situated between the Outer Banks and the mainland of North Carolina) by Sir Walter Raleigh to determine if the area would be well suited to establishing a colony. Upon their return, they delivered a positive report of the location, which included a list of the abundant natural resources surrounding the area and findings that Roanoke was better protected from the elements than the Outer Banks. They also brought back with them a Native American chief to show that relations between the tribe's people and the settlers could be peaceful. The island appeared to be a good all-around choice for a settlement, with live oaks and plenty of other trees with which to build cabins and a variety of wildlife to hunt for food. Raleigh delivered the information to Queen Elizabeth, and she granted him a charter to all the lands that he could claim in the area.

The next year Raleigh sent out a group of about 600, mostly soldiers and craftsmen, to establish the colony under the guidance of Ralph Lane, a military captain. The group met with poor results from the beginning. One of their ships struck a sandbar and tilted onto its side during their attempt to land. As a result, a good portion of their food and other supplies were lost as they tumbled into the water and sank, meaning the colony couldn't host nearly as many people as planned. In addition, they arrived in late summer and were unable to plant the crops they needed for food. The third and most disastrous occurrence was that instead of making friends with the natives, Lane fought with them and ended up killing their chief over a cup that he believed the natives had stolen. Reports state that the natives retaliated by ransacking the village and setting it on fire. This ended the opportunity to receive any help from the native tribe. With cold weather approaching, Lane and his men abandoned the area, reportedly leaving a few of the craftsmen behind. As luck or karma would have it, a ship with reinforcements and supplies arrived a week later. Fifteen men from the ship's crew were ordered to remain behind to secure the area while the captain and the rest of his crew, along with the craftsmen who didn't leave with Lane, returned to deliver this information to Raleigh in England.

Raleigh responded to the news of Lane's departure by gathering a party of 117 men, women, and children who were willing to sail from England in order to establish a permanent settlement in the New World. John White was selected to be the new governor of the charter land, which Raleigh had once proclaimed would be called the "city of Raleigh." As the group boarded the ship to sail back to the New World, White included in his party his pregnant daughter, Eleanor Dare, and her husband Annanias Dare. The native chief, who had traveled to England with the original explorers, also sailed back with the colonists.

After Lane's fiasco with the natives, Raleigh had decided that Chesapeake Bay would be a better choice for a settlement, and this was where the ship was supposed to take Governor White and his party. The Portuguese captain of the ship was first ordered to stop at Roanoke to drop off supplies and check on the men who had been left there, as well as to drop off the Native American chief at his home. The ship arrived safely in Roanoke. While there, the ship's crew discovered that the natives who had fought with Lane had also killed the 15 men who had been left behind to guard the settlement, and most everything there had been burned or destroyed with only a few bones of the dead men found scattered. It was extremely dangerous and considered uninhabitable at this time due to the ongoing battle with the local native tribe.

During the voyage to Roanoke, the ship's captain had received word that the Spanish were gearing up to fight England, and he decided that this was a golden opportunity to make a fortune pirating and looting the ships carrying cargo back and forth. He made the decision that he would not take the passengers all the way up to the Chesapeake Bay; instead, they would be left at Roanoke so that he could return to Europe. Even though the captain was aware that everyone who had previously been at Roanoke was now dead, he forced Governor White and all of the passengers off the ship and onto Roanoke Island.

The passengers scrambled to build some sort of shelter, and White immediately reached out to the Croatan people, who had been friendly with the earlier explorers. He also reached out to the other tribe that had fought with Lane. The Croatan people were friendly, but the other tribe refused to make peace with the settlers.

The colonists busied themselves trying to create shelter and unpack their belongings while the ship's crew was busy loading fresh water and other supplies back onto the ship.

On July 28, 1587, a member of White's party, George Howe, set out walking along the beach, looking to collect crabs to cook for that evening's dinner. As he was walking, he was captured and killed by the native tribe.

Afraid for their lives, the colonists asked the governor to travel back with the ship when it departed and make his way to England to ask for immediate assistance and reinforcements. This was a risky voyage, as traveling across the Atlantic Ocean in the fall was a very rough journey for ships due to storms and high waves. There was also concern about the Portuguese captain heading into battle and pirating along the way during the trip back to Europe.

Before White's departure on the ship, his daughter Eleanor gave birth to the first colonist child on August 18, 1587, on Roanoke Island. She named her child Virginia Dare. On August 27, 1587, John White sailed with the ship back to England. What happened subsequently is every father's nightmare.

Governor White just barely made it back to England. The captain noted in his ship's log that they had been lucky to find their way to the English shore. White gathered supplies and resources but could not find a captain who was willing to risk the voyage across the Atlantic during the stormy and choppy seas of the winter months. He was forced to wait, leaving his family and the colonists at the mercy of a long, cold winter with few supplies and a hostile enemy surrounding them.

In spring of the next year, White desperately tried to get back to the colonists at Roanoke. During this time the Anglo-Spanish War broke out and all available ships were being used in the battles. He managed to find two ships, which were small enough that they were deemed unable to be of any assistance in battle. As White sailed toward Roanoke, the two ships encountered Spanish pirates whose crews boarded the English ships and stole all of the cargo. Empty-handed, John White was forced back to England again to gather new resources and supplies. Due to the ongoing war, White was unable to hire a ship until three years later, in 1590, when he managed to get on board with an expedition that agreed to drop him off at Roanoke.

Three years after Eleanor gave birth to Virginia, her father landed on Roanoke Island to find everyone and everything missing. All traces of the settlement had disappeared. There was no sign of struggle, nor were there any signs of where the group had gone. His heart raced with terror. Were his daughter and granddaughter alive? Had someone taken them? There had been no way to get a direct message to them for the past three years. The colonists had no news source and relied on ships that very infrequently stopped in the area. It's highly likely that the colonists might not have known about the war that had kept White from traveling back to them. They may have presumed White to be dead or lost at sea.

Imagine how Eleanor must have felt, a new baby and practically defenseless, waiting each day in such dangerous territory, cradling her small daughter while everyone rationed the dwindling supplies. White understood this and more, realizing that his dream of starting the first settlement in the New World and bringing his daughter with him had led to her destruction.

White searched through the entire settlement, and the only clues he found was the word *CROATAN* carved into one of the trees and the letters *CRO* carved in a second tree nearby. He had asked the group to leave a sign should they be forced to move further inland and suggested that they use the sign of a Maltese cross carved in a tree should they be under attack and forced to flee for their lives.

Seeing only the word Croatan carved on the tree, his hope was that the settlers had joined the Croatan people, whose chief had been friendly to White. He hoped that they were safe with them on nearby Hatteras Island.

As he asked the ship's captain to sail to Hatteras Island, a hurricane formed in the Atlantic near the North Carolina coast, damaging the ship. The captain then ordered that the ship immediately return to England for repairs, denying White's request to sail to Hatteras Island. White returned to England with a heavy heart. By this time, he was out of money. White was never able to return to the New World to find his daughter and granddaughter.

The lost colony of Roanoke remains a mystery to this day. Theories have arisen throughout the years about what happened to the colonists. Here are a few: a hurricane swept over them, destroyed the settlement, and washed all the colonists out to sea; the hostile tribe killed them all, buried their bodies, and destroyed the settlement; the settlers, angry at what they perceived as White's desertion or death, and now hungry, alone, and cold, set out to live elsewhere and died along their journey, or they left and went to live with the Croatan tribe.

Supernatural explanations have also been raised, including werewolves attacking the group and turning the colonists into werewolves; or as they abandoned the settlement, the native tribes destroyed the camp and cursed it in order to keep others from returning. One theory posits that aliens arrived on the shore and took all of the colonists with them onto their spaceship.

The most plausible theory is that the colonists hung on for a while at the settlement, but as the cold winter blew in, they knew that between the low food supplies, angry natives, and freezing temperatures, their chances of survival were slim. Since White had befriended the chief of the Croatans, most historians believe that they reached out to the Croatans and went to live with them on Hatteras Island. This explains the Croatan message left behind on the tree for White to find.

Little physical evidence remains of the colonists from Roanoke. An eerie stillness hangs in the air and in the surrounding woods.

In 1709, John Lawson, an explorer from England, reported that he spent some time with the descendants of the Croatan tribe, who were now referred to as the Hatteras Indians. This would have been about 120 years after the birth of Virginia Dare. The explorer reported that when meeting the tribe, several of the people had very light skin and gray and blue eyes rather than brown. He reported that he had not seen this among any of the other natives he had encountered in his explorations. They told him that they were of English descent and that they had the ability to "talk in a book," which meant that they knew how to read.

More than 300 years after Eleanor and Virginia Dare's arrival in Roanoke, a North Carolina man, Hamilton MacMillan, reported that he lived near a tribe of Native Americans who claimed that their ancestors were from Roanoke. MacMillan reported that they were able to speak English and that many of them had light skin, blue eyes, and light-colored hair, and that their bone and facial structure were different in comparison to the other native tribes in North Carolina. Some people believe that this is the Lumbee Tribe, who showed English habits of living. Some of them had facial hair, including beards, which Native Americans traditionally do not have. Researchers continue to discuss and debate the lost colony of Roanoke. The most recent theory is that the settlers argued during the months after White left, some believing that he would never return and others holding out hope. The opinion is that the group broke into two parties and went their separate ways, some heading toward the Chesapeake Bay, where they had originally intended to settle, and the others assimilated into the Croatan tribe.

Historians have traced this theory, and there is some evidence that a group of settlers did arrive in Chesapeake around this time. In 1607, John Smith and the Jamestown colonists settled in the Chesapeake area, and Smith engaged in conversation with the Native Chief Powhatan. Smith reported that

Powhatan did not like new people entering his area and when they did, he attacked and killed most of them. In a conversation with Smith, Powhatan mentioned committing the murders of a group of settlers. When asked when this occurred, the date coincides with the time that a party of settlers might have arrived from Roanoke if they had left in early winter. Powhatan showed Smith proof of the colonists' existence with trinkets he had saved from the massacre. They included a musket barrel, buttons, and pieces of iron. Other historians are quick to note, though, that Smith liked to embellish his stories, as did Powhatan, and that it is likely that Powhatan had obtained the musket barrel and other pieces by trading with other tribes, and used these artifacts to intimidate and scare colonists like Smith.

Visitors to the Roanoke settlement can see the small remnants left behind by the colonists. Ghosts are seen walking around where the fort stood and often appear standing along the beach, perhaps hoping to see a ship on the horizon bringing much-needed supplies and reinforcements. Theories suggest that one of the ghosts may be the colonist George Howe, who was attacked and killed by the natives while he walked the beach looking for crabs. Other ghosts may include the 15 men who were left behind to guard the settlement and were murdered by the angry natives.

During my research of the Lost Colony, I had the opportunity to speak with Anne Poole, cofounder and research director of The Lost Colony Research Group. Anne and I were able to discuss many of the haunted sites in North Carolina, as she also leads the Carolina Ghost Hunters, which researches paranormal events around the state. Anne arranged the overnight ghost hunt in the state capitol building during the night that my research group, The Rowan Society, attended and had paranormal experiences of our own.

I spoke with Anne about her ongoing research and archaeological work at the Lost Colony area with cofounder Roberta

Estes. The two women work with a team of archaeologists from England who are studying the site, and together they are determined to solve the mystery of what happened to Virginia Dare and the Lost Colony. They're doing some incredible research, including using DNA from the descendants of the colonist families in England in order to test families in North Carolina who may be genetically linked.

For Anne, researching the Lost Colony became a passion for her at the age of 10, when her parents first brought her to the area to show her the history of North Carolina and the Lost Colony. She was hooked on the mystery from that point and has dedicated a generous portion of her time to researching the history of the Dare family and the other colonists. I asked Anne which theory she subscribed to as to where the colonists went, and she feels they stuck together and went to live with the Croatan tribe. She said from a logical standpoint, they were strangers in a new world, and there is safety in numbers. They were facing the unknown, as well as hostile native tribes, swamps, poor maps, high heat and humidity that they had not been exposed to in England, as well as the threat of alligators, bears, wolves, poisonous snakes, and other predators. She went on to explain that there's also the evidence of Croatan written on the tree. She pointed out that if the people had headed to Chesapeake Bay, wouldn't they have written the word Chesapeake on the tree? It certainly makes the most sense of all.

As Anne and I continued to chat, an interesting thing occurred. I saw a Native American man standing behind her in spirit. The more she talked about the Lost Colony and the Croatan, the stronger his energy became. His presence was so powerful that I felt compelled to mention this to Anne. I described the Native American man to her and told her that I felt he was a protective guide for her, and beyond that, I had the impression that he was helping her on her quest to find the evidence of the Lost Colony. As I spoke to this man in spirit, he told me that Anne is a descendant of the Lost Colony and it is part of her destiny to assist in finding what happened to the colonists. It appeared to me that he intends to stay with her on every step of this journey until it is complete. As I shared what I had seen with Anne, it surprised her a bit, and then she shared with me a story of a place she had been only a short while back where she had been giving a lecture on the history of North Carolina. After the talk, a woman approached her and said that she had seen a Native American man standing behind Anne during her talk. My having seen the same spirit during my conversation with Anne served to confirm what she saw. It certainly left me with the understanding that Anne may very well be the person to discover the evidence that so many have looked for, as I believe her to be one of the descendants of these colonists.

Finishing up my conversation with Anne, I thanked her for her time, and we discussed holding a ghost-hunting event in the future for other paranormal researchers and interested people who wish to explore North Carolina. She also confirmed for me the history of what I had found in my research about the Lost Colony. She then shared that she had experienced some supernatural experiences in some of the other places I was writing about, including the Mordecai House in Raleigh. While Anne and her daughter were there, her daughter had a ghost touch her and blow in her ear while they were in Mary Turk's room on the Mordecai House tour.

There's so much still to uncover about the Lost Colony of Roanoke. One thing is for sure: when you visit the Lost Colony area, it feels eerie and isolated. It looks open and unprotected, and the woods surrounding you feel dangerous. The area remains much the same as it was when the settlers arrived, and you'll get a good idea of what it was like to live at that time.

I enjoyed the natural beauty and scenic views of the area. At the same time, I tried to imagine what it was like to be Eleanor Dare, pregnant in a new world and facing starvation, exposure to the elements, and the constant threat of being attacked and killed. I also wondered how John White had been given the position and responsibility of being governor, as research shows that he was an artist by trade.

As I tuned in to the energy around the area, I thought I would sense fear, but it felt more like nervous tension, like anxiety. The daily struggle of waiting, hoping, and wondering if help would come or if they would be attacked by natives one night would be so much to bear on a daily basis. The area has a haunted, lonely feeling that still remains today. With that much anxiety, fear, and death, it's not surprising that ghost stories continue to be reported.

The Roanoke Island Historical Association presents an outdoor drama each summer portraying what happened to the settlers of the lost colony. The scene is striking, set outdoors in the area where the settlement once stood, using the Atlantic Ocean as the backdrop.

In my conversation with Anne Poole about the surrounding area, she shared with me another haunted story, which she has personally experienced on Roanoke Island. It began on Mother Vineyard Road, where the oldest grapevine in the United States is reported to exist. When the colonists first arrived at Roanoke, they reported that the island was covered with wild grapes, which may have been scuppernong vines. Mother's Vineyard is a private location that has continued to produce grapes from this vine for more than 400 years, surviving explorers, colonists, the elements, and the Civil War. Over the years, locals and visitors have reported seeing a ghost man with an eerie glow riding a bike on this road. When the man appears, many report also hearing a cat scream and the ringing of a bike bell. They also describe some of the activities as "hoodoos." Hoodoos are small, dark creatures that appear as shadowy figures and are sometimes mischievous. Many locals believe that the ghost riding the bicycle is a hoodoo. All of the people who encounter this hoodoo energy describe it as feeling ancient and intensely overpowering.

Anne was called in to investigate the hoodoo with her paranormal research group, and she interviewed several witnesses who personally attested to seeing the ghostly man, including two college students. During her investigation, Anne sensed the presence of a woman in the area who she describes as a granny-type character. The woman appeared to be a caretaker, watching over the land and the Mother Vineyard. While she didn't experience the hoodoo while investigating, she did come away with the impression that the area is haunted by several beings.

When you plan your visit to the Lost Colony of Roanoke, remember that the actual area is quite bare. The Lost Colony is open to visit, but there is not much here at the site. Mother's Vineyard is private property and not open to visitors, but you can drive down the road to see if a hoodoo appears to you one night. The nearby town of Manteo offers accommodations and restaurants. While you're this far out on the Outer Banks, you might also enjoy driving another half hour to Rodanthe, where the movie *Nights in Rodanthe* was filmed, starring Richard Gere. The movie was based on the book of the same title by Nicholas Sparks.

BEAUTIFUL NELL CROPSEY STILL WAITS IN ELIZABETH CITY

Elizabeth City's most famous ghost is the beautiful 19-year-old Nell Cropsey, who mysteriously disappeared from her home along the Pasquotank River in 1901. Nell had moved to Elizabeth City in 1898 with her family from Brooklyn, New York. She was reported to be very attractive and had a long line of male suitors in town openly desiring to court her. During this time, she was dating Jim Wilcox, the son of the local county sheriff. For months Nell had been waiting for Jim to ask her to marry him, but he appeared to being making no move toward asking for her hand. In an attempt to provoke Jim into popping the question, Nell began flirting with other men.

One evening Jim stopped by to see Nell at the Cropsey family home. Nell's sister reported that Nell and Jim began arguing about Nell spending time with another man. As the argument grew more heated, Jim asked Nell to step outside of the house onto the front porch, where they continued arguing into the late evening. Before heading off to bed, the sister went to check on them, only to find no sight of Nell or Jim. A few moments later, a neighbor came running up to the house shouting that someone had been in the backyard trying to steal the Cropsey's family pig.

The hunt began for Nell. Police searched the city and throughout the county for a month, and even dragged the river behind the Cropsey home to look for her body, all to no avail. During this time, her father received a strange letter postmarked Utica, New York, which said that Nell had seen a man trying to steal the family's pig and that when she had tried to stop him, he had hit her on the head with a stick and carried her off in a rowboat. The letter also marked an area in the river where Nell's body would be found.

BEAUTIFUL NELL CROPSEY STILL WAITS IN ELIZABETH CITY (CONTINUED)

It was more than 37 days before Nell was found floating in the Pasquotank River. Her grieving mother had kept a nightly vigil for her daughter and would walk around the backyard each night for hours. One moonlit evening while standing in the backyard, she saw something white floating in the river and called for help to have it pulled from the water. It was the body of Nell, located in the area where the mysterious letter from New York had said it would be found.

Nell's body was placed in the nearby Cropsey boathouse, and the autopsy was conducted there on-site. The coroner found that she died not from drowning but from blunt force trauma to her head. Jim Wilcox was charged with the crime and sentenced to death, but a mistrial was declared by the North Carolina Supreme Court due to public interference with the investigation, including the organization of a lynch mob that wanted to take matters into its own hands.

Jim was tried again in a different county for the crime, convicted of second-degree murder, and sentenced to 30 years in prison. He only served a few years of his sentence before being pardoned by the governor due to the political connections of his family. Upon his release, he immediately returned to live in Elizabeth City until his death by suicide.

Reports state that Nell's home in Elizabeth City is haunted by her ghost, which has been seen in her bedroom, on the front porch, and along the river. The home is a private residence and is not open to the public. A walking ghost tour is held each October in which you can hear the full story of Nell's ghost sightings and see other haunted areas of Elizabeth City.

CHAPTER 6

CRESWELL

THE GHOSTS OF SOMERSET PLACE

In 1865, more than 850 enslaved people worked at Somerset Place. At that time, the plantation grounds included more than 100,000 acres of farmland, woodland, and swampland.

Somerset Place is an antebellum plantation that in the 1850s once covered more than 100,000 acres and was considered to be one of North Carolina's largest plantations. Throughout the years of its operation, reports state that more than 850 enslaved people worked and lived there.

Before Somerset Place was built, the land was a 200,000-

acre swampy area referred to by the colonists as the Great Eastern Dismal or the Great Alligator Dismal. The swamp was considered so foreboding that most men didn't dare enter the area. Along with the dangers of quicksand, the land was inhabited by wild animals, including wolves, panthers, bears, and a variety of poisonous snakes.

Eventually, in the mid-1700s, two men did finally dare to venture deep into the swampland. After a long day of trudging through the murky waters and treacherous woods, one of the men, Benjamin Tarkington, climbed up a tree to see what lay beyond where they stood. What he saw was a large lake. Still up in the tree, he yelled down to his companion, Josiah Phelps, that a lake was up ahead. Phelps ran through the brush and into the lake and claimed it as his own, naming it Lake Phelps. At this time in history, the first person to enter the water asserted the right to claim and name the lake. The discovery of fresh water suggested that the area could be farmed if there were a way to dry out the swampland surrounding it.

In 1787, Josiah Collins moved from England and developed the area by draining the swamp, creating farmland that could be used to grow a variety of crops in the fertile soil. He built Somerset Place, naming the plantation after the county he had moved from in England. He forced 100 slaves to dig a 6-mile canal, which connected Lake Phelps with the Scuppernong River. He also designed a system of canals to carry water across the plantation in order to irrigate his crops. This led to Somerset Place becoming one of the most successful plantations in North Carolina, with crops of wheat, rice, and corn.

Years later, Josiah Collins III inherited the plantation from his namesake grandfather. He was living in New York at the time, where he had completed his education. He had also gained a reputation for being domineering and aggressive. During this time, he met and married Mary Riggs from Newark, New Jersey, and they moved to live at Somerset Place.

Josiah enjoyed entertaining and was known to have a number of large parties and social events at Somerset, including three-day festivals at Christmas. For the wedding of his son, Josiah IV, he had the entire home redecorated and a special cake shipped in express from New York. Josiah and Mary had four sons during their first six years of marriage, eventually reaching a total of six boys. Tragically, three of the sons died in accidents on the plantation.

Around 1840, two of Josiah and Mary's sons (Edward and Hugh) were swimming in the canal in front of the house, along with two slave boys (Zacharias and Anderson). The details are lost to history, but all four boys drowned one day together in the canal. A third son later died on the plantation, but his cause of death is unknown.

Under the direction of Josiah III, the plantation reached its greatest height in production, with more than 300 slaves working the fields. Of them, 60% were women, and they labored in the fields with the men.

In 1860, Mary suffered a stroke, leaving her without the ability to write or speak, and three years later Josiah Collins died suddenly when the family was forced to leave the plantation during the Civil War. After the war, the Collins's fortune was gone. Two of the sons returned with their mother to the plantation, where Mary died in 1872. Her boys then sold the property at auction, due to the amount of debt owed on the property after the war. It went through several owners before the Federal Farm Security Administration purchased it in 1937 and turned it into a historic park.

The plantation now sits on 8 acres of land surrounding state-operated Pettigrew Park. The park is named for General Pettigrew, who led his Confederate troops into battle at Gettysburg; he was the nearest neighbor to the Collins family and reportedly did not care for them or how they conducted themselves. His gravesite is located near Somerset off the old carriage road.

Somerset is reported to be home to many ghosts. It is said that Mary never recovered from the drowning of her two sons in the canal and that she can still be heard crying and mourning for them. The ghosts of the four boys are also seen on the property and heard crying for help. The nearby gravesite of General Pettigrew is also reportedly haunted. He appears in a gray mist that can be seen among the trees and around the property.

Some reports state that several ghosts on the land are former slaves who haunt the plantation. One of the saddest stories is that of an enslaved woman, Rebecca Drew, who attempted to run away one evening and was caught. The stories say that she was sent to work at Somerset in the fields at the age of 15. She had lived with her parents at another plantation before being sent to Somerset. She desperately missed being with her parents, which prompted her attempt to run away in hopes to see them at the other plantation.

When she was captured, she was placed in arm and leg stocks overnight as a punishment. During the night it was so cold that she lost circulation in her legs and her feet were badly frostbitten. As a result, both of her feet had to be amputated. She somehow survived the amputation and found a crude and undoubtedly painful way to continue to walk around on her stumps. In this condition, she was forced to continue to work on the plantation.

There are also reports of slaves who attempted to poison the overseer, whom they said was very cruel to all of them. The slaves who were caught with the poison were sold immediately at auction and forced to leave their family members behind at Somerset.

The atrocities that were committed during this horrific time in history still weigh heavily on this land. If you decide to visit the area, please proceed with great respect and intention to learn and understand, rather than attempting to contact spirits who have suffered greatly.

The outer quarters are one of the areas where active hauntings are still reported.

When visiting the location, it feels like ancient land. I didn't detect much energy around the home itself; rather it was in the land where I felt the most energy. I would describe it as shamanistic in nature, perhaps originating with ancient native tribes and their rituals, and later by the enslaved people who brought their West African religious practices with them. The trees here feel very old and they hold the energy of this land. They bore witness to all that occurred during the plantation years and the Civil War.

Local stories state that the sound of a woman screaming can often be heard in the area, and they attribute it to Mary, screaming about the drowning of her two sons. Some people say that she screamed for days during her grief over the loss of her sons and that she continued to do this over the years. When a large amount of sadness and negative energy is expressed in the home over and over, it creates an energy imprint that can be heard at times, like a tape recorder playing something over and over. In these cases, it's not the actual ghost who is still there in the home, but rather a recording of that energy that can still be heard and on some occasions seen, as if watching a film of the event. Mary's ghost has not been reported as appearing to anyone—only the sound of her screams and crying over the death of her sons.

While I'm not surprised to hear the reports of a woman screaming in the area, I feel that most of the paranormal experiences occur on the land during late moonlit nights, when the wind whispers through the trees and the spirits come forward to tell their tales.

Lake Phelps is also a local mystery. It is the second-largest natural lake in the state and is reported to be more than 12,000 years old. Scientists have not been able to confirm its origin. Many theories have been proposed, including meteor showers, underground springs, and glacial activity. The lake is 5 miles across and has a maximum depth of only 9 feet; the water is clear, while all of the streams surrounding it remain murky like the surrounding swampy areas. There is no outside source found for the lake, so it appears that all of the water comes from rainfall. The lake continues to mystify scientists. It is also being studied to determine what properties in the water provide it with such a high capacity to preserve wood and how so many different species came to live in this environment, which normally would not support them in a comfortable habitat.

Artifacts have been found near the lake dating back to 8,000 BCE. More than 30 dugout canoes made from cypress have been pulled from the lake, one carbon-dated to more than 4,400 years ago. One of the canoes is more than 36 feet in length, and it is believed that the native tribes would sink the canoes to store them and then would retrieve them when they returned to the area each year.

Lake Phelps is considered to be a sacred site by some Native American tribes, and legends state that it is the home to ancient spirits who protect the land. The natives who fished there believed that you could take the food that you needed from the lake, as long as you gave thanks and offerings to the spirits.

As colonists began to settle in North Carolina, it was years before the lake was known to them. Even when the lake was discovered, the colonists still were unable to venture deep into this area for many more years, as they didn't understand the terrain very well in comparison to the natives who had been using the area for centuries.

While visiting, we stopped for a bite to eat, and I chatted with some people at a café, asking them if they knew of any ghost stories at Lake Phelps. An older gentleman told me that there is a local legend about the lake. According to his report, in the 1880s, there was a man who chose to live out near Lake Phelps in a small cabin with his dog. He kept to himself with the exception of traveling to a trading post on occasion to gather supplies. One cold winter day, he visited the trading post with a story that concerned all who heard his tale. The man had been out hunting near Lake Phelps, and he came across an all-white deer. Taking aim with his rifle, he shot and killed the deer, watching it fall to the ground. As the man walked toward the carcass on the ground, it disappeared before his eyes. He also heard strange noises coming from the woods, and a strong wind began to whirl around him. Terrified, he headed back through the woods by the lake to his cabin. As he arrived at his cabin, a mist surrounded him and he heard voices whispering to him. He also saw blue orbs of light appearing over the lake, floating in the air above the water. At this point, he was terrified, and he ran from his cabin and kept going until he arrived at the trading post to tell his story.

It seems that he had attempted to kill one of the guardian spirits of the land, which had taken the form of a white deer. By doing so, he had awoken and angered the ancient spirits. After telling his story at the trading post, he was advised by the people there not to return as they feared for his safety, but he insisted that he needed to go back home. The man was never seen again, and eventually a search party was sent to look for him. He was found lying dead in the woods, appearing to have died from a terrible fright.

No one knows what happened to the man or how he died, but others who venture into the woods near Lake Phelps at night report hearing strange sounds and howls, as well as several voices whispering in the wind. Many people also report seeing a mist that rises from the lake and then spreads out into the woods. On several nights this is also followed by seeing blue orbs that hover and float across the water.

TOUCHED BY THE LADY IN BLACK

The Fayetteville Women's Club is located in the historic Sandford House on Heritage Square, which was built in 1797. Apparitions of a lady dressed in black have been reported in the house since 1900 and are still being reported by some of the ladies of the Women's Club. The "lady in black" frequently appears on the stairs, and many believe her to be Margaret Sandford, who lived in the house in the 1800s. But others believe a much different tale.

One evening at the Sandford House, a Confederate soldier was visiting his true love. During this visit, news arrived stating that Union soldiers from Sherman's army were close to taking over Fayetteville. Hearing the news, the young soldier was desperate to get to his regiment in time to help protect the bridge over the Cape Fear River.

The Sandford House had a secret tunnel inside that led to the Cape Fear River. The soldier's beloved led him to the hidden tunnel entrance so that he could reach his men and help protect Fayetteville. She wished him a safe and speedy return, and night after night, she waited for him to return to her through the tunnel entrance. The battle raged on, and the young soldier was never seen again, nor was his body ever found.

When the ghost of this young lady is seen, she appears in a long black dress, which all the ladies wore at that time as the color of mourning for their lost husbands, sons, and lovers. Reports state that the lady in black is often seen walking up and down the stairs, anxiously waiting for her lover to return. Many witnesses have reported seeing her in several locations throughout the home, and they often feel her hand on their shoulder as she reaches out to them from behind. The legend states that some of the ladies of the Fayetteville Women's Club

TOUCHED BY THE LADY IN BLACK (CONTINUED)

believe that she touches them gently to have them turn to face her so that she can see who is in her home. Perhaps she also hopes that they will have some news for her regarding the soldier's return.

The lady in black is reported to be gentle and sad. She appears to be patiently waiting and grieving. Her state of dress indicates that she may have received news that all the men in the battle were confirmed dead, but since his body was never found, perhaps she has a glimmer of hope that he may have survived and against all odds will return to her one day.

CHAPTER 7

TARBORO

SOUTHERN HOSPITALITY EXTENDS INTO THE AFTERLIFE AT THE BLOUNT-BRIDGERS HOUSE

Tarboro was established in 1760 along the Tar River and is located in what is described as the Inner Banks area of North Carolina. Originally it was referred to as Tawboro, *taw* being a native Tuscarora word referring to "the river of health."

My most favorite part of Tarboro is the historic area, which is a 45-block district with more than 300 residential homes, historic churches, and many 19th-century buildings still standing and in use. Tarboro also has a 15-acre park with war memorials and a town common.

When I visited Tarboro, the town was celebrating its 250th anniversary. The celebration included a variety of events based on the town's history. Driving around the Tarboro historic commons, one senses how ripe it must be for ghostly activity. In 1863, 800 Union soldiers engaged in a five-day attack on Greenville, Tarboro, and Rocky Mount, destroying steamboats and supplies in Tarboro. As we've already seen in these investigations, the Civil War made its mark across North Carolina, and many ghosts remain to tell the tale.

Sitting within the historic district is the Blount-Bridgers House, which was a Federal-style plantation home built in 1808 by Thomas Blount. Blount built the plantation, originally called the Grove, on 296 acres of land. Throughout

The house boasts a substantial art collection and many 19th-century items, including household goods and military uniforms.

the years, the house seemed to welcome and favor military men. Thomas Blount lived in the home from 1808 to 1812, Colonel Louis Dicken Wilson lived there from 1831 to 1847, and Colonel John Bridgers lived in the home from 1850 to 1880.

During the American Revolution, many of the locals fought valiantly in the war, including Thomas Blount, who became a prisoner of war in England. He was eventually freed and returned to North Carolina to help create one of the largest shipping companies in the late 18th century and later served in the U.S. House of Representatives. Colonel Wilson served in the North Carolina Senate and fought in the Mexican–American War, and Colonel Bridgers is best known for his service as a commandant in the Civil War, where he served at Fort Macon.

The Blount-Bridgers House served as a public library and a dance studio before it was turned into a museum in 1979. It features a nice collection of 19th-century furniture along with the art collection of Tarboro-born Hobson Pittman. The home is welcoming with wraparound porches, which I love; I could spend an afternoon here just relaxing and chatting on the porch.

The parlor and the art rooms on the first floor are where some people have reported feeling a ghostly presence.

While taking the tour of the Blount-Bridgers House, we were guided to two areas of the home where a female ghost has been seen and felt by visitors and staff. Many presume the ghost to be Jackie Blount, and she is most often seen in the parlor and the art room displaying Hobson Pittman's art. Apparently a lady of good taste, she has a love and appreciation of art and likes to show her Southern hospitality by greeting guests who visit her home.

During my research and conversations with local residents, I learned that the ghost, Jackie (Mary Jacqueline Sumner Blount), was the wife of Thomas Blount and part of the Sumner family connected to the Mordecai House in Raleigh. I write more about the Mordecai House in the Central Carolina section of this book, as it is also haunted.

This led me to wonder: Do ghosts visit all of their family homes and haunts, much as they used to travel back then between their winter and summer homes? Could the ghosts of the Blount-Bridgers House also be haunting the Mordecai House? Did Jackie still spend time between the two cities, coming and going according to social occasions in spirit, and was John Bridgers enjoying the Blount-Bridgers home in the afterlife while also spending time checking on his troops at Fort Macon, which is also haunted?

Most likely, we'll never know for sure, though it is interesting to ponder. I also find it fascinating that the more I travel and investigate throughout the state, the more connections I find between haunted areas, historic sites, and family trees. Some people leave such a lasting impression in life that their presence continues to be felt in every location where they lived, fought, and loved.

While visiting Tarboro, I also learned about the gravesite of Civil War General William Dorsey Pender, who is buried in Calvary Churchyard in Tarboro. He was fatally wounded during the Battle of Gettysburg. Many locals say that his ghost is still around today and has been seen in both the church graveyard and in the town commons area. He's reported to be cordial and a true Southern gentleman. What I found most romantic about his story is that the letters that the general wrote to his wife were collected and published almost 100 years after his death in a book titled, *The General to His Lady: The Civil War Letters of William Dorsey Pender to Fanny Pender.*

THE WANDERING GHOSTS OF NAGS HEAD

The Outer Banks of North Carolina are incredibly haunted. With so many shipwrecks and people lost at sea, ghostly images are often seen walking along the shore. While the shifting sandbars and unpredictable currents caused the majority of shipwrecks along the coast, many others were caused by pirate attacks at sea. The legend of Nags Head reveals an entirely new threat to sailors, what some might describe as the darker side of necessity.

According to local legend, wannabe sea pirates who were landlubbers by day wickedly designed their own special style of pirating. They would gather their horses and hang lanterns around their necks and walk the horses up and down the dunes at night, attempting to lure ships into the area. The lights hanging from the horses' heads led the merchant ships off course, as it appeared that the lights were coming from ships close to the shore. As the ships changed course and headed toward the lights, they ran aground on sandbars. The "land pirates" would then storm the ships and steal the cargo. The legends state that the coastal area where this occurred was named "Nags Head" due to the reputation gained by the land pirates' fast footwork with the horses and the lanterns around their necks. Others claim that the town was named by English settlers from a similar area in the Isles of Scilly off the English coast.

Nags Head was a popular vacation destination for local plantation owners who lived farther inland in North Carolina and sought to escape the oppressive heat, humidity, and threat of malaria from mosquitoes in the summer months. A resort called the Nags Head Hotel was built in the 1850s, and 20 years later the hotel, located near Jockey's Ridge, literally sank beneath the shifting sands. Local legends state that the

THE WANDERING GHOSTS OF NAGS HEAD (CONTINUED)

hotel remains intact 100 feet below the surface. The cottages of that period still stand and are referred to as the "Unpainted Aristocracy."

Ghosts often appear all along the shore of Nags Head. Some say they are the crews of the ships plundered by the land pirates, and others say that they are former guests of the hotel, looking for it below the sand.

A third theory for the ghostly appearances states that many of the historic cottages in the area had porches built onto their homes using lumber salvaged from shipwrecks that washed in from the coast. The ghosts connected to the lumber from these ships now remain near the homes. They are still looking for the rest of their ships to wash up on the shores, along with their lost treasures and belongings.

Regardless of which ghosts are roaming the area, a visit to the Outer Banks and Nags Head provides many haunting opportunities.

CHAPTER 8

CAPE HATTERAS

FULL MOON HIGHLIGHTS THE GHOSTS OF THE CAPE HATTERAS LIGHTHOUSE

Built in 1870, the Cape Hatteras Lighthouse is the tallest brick lighthouse in the United States. The beacon of light can be seen from a distance of 20 miles by sea.

Paranormal researchers have to be ready for anything and everything when ghost hunting. They often have to deal with weather issues, equipment failures, as well as physical challenges as they're often tromping through dense woods and other rough terrain.

Walking through the battleship USS *North Carolina* is a bit of a maze, and it's hard work climbing up and down the iron ladders that are euphemistically called "stairs." As I was moving through the ship, it was readily apparent that trying to bring a film crew on board to run cables throughout the ship would be quite a task. Shows like *Ghost Hunters* have an established crew that sets up the monitors, cameras, and equipment, hoping to catch paranormal activity on film. They've visited the USS *North Carolina,* and I can imagine how hard the TV crew had to work in order to prepare for that investigation.

After the USS *North Carolina* tour, I headed out to see the Cape Hatteras Lighthouse. If you've ever been to North Carolina, you'll recognize it as the state symbol, painted in a signature swirl of black and white. It's quite spectacular to see firsthand. Some people describe it as the biggest barber pole they have ever seen.

I like the swirl-style painting of the lighthouse. It's one of those things that I call a happy accident. The lighthouse was supposed to have been painted in a diamond pattern, but the engineer was confused by the plans and he designed the spiral instead, making the structure very distinctive. The lighthouse was built to warn sailors of the Diamond Shoals, which are sandbars that shift often and can extend more than 14 feet outward from the shore at Cape Hatteras. In addition, it is in this area of the Atlantic that the Gulf Stream collides with the colder Labrador current. Often, the end result of the collision between the warm Gulf current and the cold Labrador current is the creation of powerful ocean storms and high sea swells. These sandbars and tricky currents have sunk many ships and given North Carolina the nickname of the "Graveyard of the Atlantic."

When you arrive at the Cape Hatteras Lighthouse, the first thought that hits you is how tall it is and how small you feel standing next to it. The second thought is that you want to climb it! It's there, it must be climbed, and the view from the top is a must-see.

The lighthouse has 257 iron stairs arranged in a spiral. Climbing to the top of the lighthouse is equivalent to climbing a 12-story building. It's noisy, as many people are climbing to the top with you. Their shoes clang on the iron steps, there's no air-conditioning, and it gets pretty hot and sticky fast. There are a couple of windows in the lighthouse, but for the most part, the lighting is dim. As you continue the climb, you encounter people coming back down, and there's a bit of a tussle as there is only a handrail on one side to hold onto. You become very friendly with strangers as you negotiate to allow them to pass by you. Luckily there is a landing every 31 steps to stop and wait when large groups are coming down.

I visited during the day to see the lighthouse. This is a must-do, as the view from the top is spectacular.

In 1999, the lighthouse was moved from its original location. Wow! Can you imagine the engineering feat it took to move a lighthouse? Erosion from the waves and shifting sands threatened to destroy the foundation in its former location, and the decision had to be made to either attempt to move the lighthouse to safety or to watch it disappear as the sand shifted and the ocean claimed it as its own. The lighthouse, along with the keeper's house, was moved 2,900 feet away. This process took a painstakingly slow 23 days to complete.

In 1999, the Cape Hatteras Lighthouse had to be relocated due to erosion around its shore from the Atlantic Ocean. Ghostly sightings continue to be reported, as it seems the ghosts are connected to the lighthouse, regardless of where it sits on land.

Given that the lighthouse has been the guardian to the Graveyard of the Atlantic, it's no surprise to find that it's also extremely haunted.

One haunting tale is the story of the *Carroll A. Deering*, a sailing ship that was returning from Barbados on its way to Hampton Roads, Virginia. On January 31, 1921, the *Carroll A. Deering* was found run aground on the Diamond Shoals off the coast of Cape Hatteras. The ship was a five-masted schooner built in 1919 in Bath, Maine. The Coast Guard was called, and guardsmen sailed out to inspect the ship, which was found empty with the exception of several very hungry cats. The investigation found that a dinner had recently been prepared and the dishes were still on the table. The ship was in good order, but the lifeboats were missing.

What would cause the captain and crew to abandon the ship in such a hurry when it was in good working order? Why would they leave their cats behind? The research indicates that the crew left in a panic, as if they were afraid of something. Along with their dinner, they left a perfectly good boat in running order. They didn't even stop to lower the sails. There had to have been something extreme to cause a captain and his crew to leave a ship in that condition, especially when they were facing freezing cold weather and high sea swells in January on the Atlantic Ocean.

Upon further investigation, the Coast Guard found that all of the anchors were missing from the ship, along with some papers and personal belongings of the captain and crew. The vessel remained stuck on the shoals until it was towed away in March. What remained of the ship was blown up with dynamite. I found that fact surprising: Why would evidence of an unsolved mystery be deliberately destroyed? In addition, why wouldn't any part of the ship be salvaged for future use elsewhere?

Reports state that in April of the same year, a North Carolina resident found a bottle washed up on shore with a note inside stating that the captain and crew had been captured by pirates. The letter was later determined to be a hoax.

The following month, the wife of the ship's captain visited Washington and asked then–Secretary of Commerce Herbert Hoover to investigate what had happened to her husband and his crew. He agreed to look into the matter after his research showed that nine other ships had also disappeared in the same area. The FBI was sent to investigate the matter in July 1921. The investigators returned with reports describing theories foul play, including attacks by pirates, attacks by rumrunners, and the possibility of mutiny.

The theory of mutiny was tossed aside. The seas are so rough in that part of the Atlantic in January that it would be a suicide mission by the crew and the worst timing on their part. The ship was only a day or two away from reaching Virginia, where it was scheduled to dock. Regardless of the circumstances, it's highly unlikely that a crew would have picked this location where so many ships are known to wreck. In addition, a mutinous crew would have tossed the captain overboard and most likely would have continued on with the ship, sailing to a port in another country.

Foul play with pirates or rumrunners also seemed unlikely as there were no dead bodies left on the ship, as well as no signs of struggle or blood. The ship's log, the lifeboats, and the navigation equipment were missing and never found. Although there was a detailed investigation, all of the leads turned up empty. To this day, the mystery continues.

After the ship ran aground, witnesses in the area began to report hearing people screaming for help near the shore. The reports state that when witnesses hear the screaming, they go to investigate, but no one is ever seen. Some of these reports say that several people have heard a man scream over and over that a monster is coming for him.

Some locals think that a ghost appeared on the ship, perhaps one of the pirates from the many sunken ships that lay below the ocean near Cape Hatteras. Perhaps these pirate ghosts boarded the ship as the crew prepared their dinner and scared them out of their minds, to the point that they jumped into the lifeboats and abandoned ship, leaving everything behind. In their fear and perhaps demise, it appears that they may have joined the ghosts and now walk the beaches beside them.

The most famous ghost on Cape Hatteras is called the Gray Man. He appears to people to warn them when a hurricane or severe storm is heading toward the island. Some say that he is a sailor who drowned during a storm and now warns others of impending storms. Others say that he was in love with a local girl and in his haste to get back to her took a shortcut with his traveling companions through a swampy area and drowned in quicksand.

The legend states that the local woman was devastated upon hearing the news of his death. Each night for weeks she walked the beach in sorrow and grief. One night as she walked along the beach, he appeared to her as the Gray Man and told her that she needed to leave immediately because a hurricane was coming. She ran home and told her family, who believed her, and they left right away and went inland.

The next morning, a hurricane hit the island and destroyed many of the homes there, but her home was spared. The legend states that if the Gray Man appears to you and you heed his advice to leave, then your house will be spared by the storm. Reports continue to be shared by locals who say they have seen the man appear before them out of thin air. He warns them of an approaching storm and then quickly disappears.

Other reports include seeing a strange-colored brown pelican in a ghostly form that appears to warn locals about incoming storms. Some say that the phantom bird may be a companion of the Gray Man.

There are also reports of a lady of Spanish descent, dressed all in black, who walks along the shore by the lighthouse. Her clothes are wet and hang on her body. By most accounts, it appears that she drowned in a shipwreck. Most reports state that she is angry and is looking for something that she never can find. At times it appears that she screams and wails like a banshee. Perhaps she's searching for a lost treasure or her jewels that were lost at sea. She is often seen on full-moon nights, and I imagine that the view from the top of the lighthouse might provide a vantage point to watch the surrounding shore for ghosts walking along the beach.

Shadow people are also reported to appear near the vicinity of the lighthouse and inside on the staircase. Some paranormal researchers think shadow people may be a specific type of ghost, while others surmise that they are dark and malicious entities traveling from the various supernatural realms into the earth plane.

Shadow people are not considered to be friendly, and when they are seen, they often do not have faces. They appear in a human shape but are not completely formed. The two most popular theories about the shadow people fall into two camps: one is that the shadow people are thought-forms, which are created when deep trauma has occurred in the area and the emotional intensity is so strong that it gives life to a thought form, a tulpa, which then haunts the area.

The other theory is that they are not from this world but are attracted to areas where negative experiences have caused a great amount of trauma and pain. They enter the earth plane to feed on the energy of this trauma and the energy from grieving victims. For this reason, shadow people are often seen in cemeteries.

Given the hundreds of shipwrecks around Cape Hatteras Lighthouse and the Diamond Shoals and the ghosts who walk the beach, many of whom still lay in their physical form under the sea in sunken ships, the entire area is a restless place and ripe for paranormal activity.

In addition, there are many reports of unmarked graves in the area around the lighthouse, leading to the potential for other undocumented ghosts as well. While walking around the lighthouse and the shore, you can feel the sadness in the air. You don't earn the nickname Graveyard of the Atlantic without having more than a few ghosts around with unfinished business, some looking for their treasure; some trying to escape what horrified them; and others, like the Gray Man, trying to protect the local residents from further harm.

THE LONELY GHOSTS OF FOSCUE PLANTATION

Simon Foscue once made his living serving as a justice of the peace. He later expanded his career by building the Foscue Plantation House in 1804. At one time, the plantation spanned more than 10,000 acres. During the Civil War, the Foscue Plantation was taken over by Union troops and used as a hospital. Historic records show that in this area of North Carolina along the Trent River, Union troops destroyed all other houses in the vicinity. For a long period of time after the war, Foscue Plantation was the only house still standing in the area.

Traveling out to see the plantation, I couldn't help but think about its history, a place of bondage for 40 slaves who worked on the plantation; a hospital for soldiers, many of whom undoubtedly died on the grounds; and a house ransacked by Union soldiers and then left alone, depleted and desolate after the war. The Civil War may have been the event most directly responsible for creating so many ghosts in the South.

As I approached the plantation home, it appeared smaller to me than I had pictured it on the ride. While it certainly isn't a small cottage by any means (the house has three floors and a basement), it just seemed too small to have held such sorrow.

The home itself is beautifully restored, and the architecture is quite interesting, including the bricks of the home, which were made by hand on the property. The house has remained in family ownership for many generations, which is a testament to the strength and commitment of the family, who undoubtedly had to struggle to make ends meet for some time after the war.

The small graveyard behind the home includes the grave of John Foscue and reminds one of the many deaths this place had seen over the years. Iron gates greeted me at the entrance to the plantation.

THE LONELY GHOSTS OF FOSCUE PLANTATION (CONTINUED)

There are several magical theories about iron, which state that the material can be used as a barrier to contain spirits in one space.

Apparitions of wounded soldiers and enslaved people are reported around the home and grounds. While walking around the area, I could feel a presence watching me. It felt like a guardian, who kept a watchful eye and was still attached to the land. It's hard for me to shake the sadness I felt on this land; it still haunts me to this day.

CHAPTER 9

NEW BERN

THE ATTMORE-OLIVER HOUSE AND THE WEEPING ARCH OF CEDAR GROVE

Originally built in 1790 and expanded in 1834, the Attmore-Oliver House has a long history of hauntings.

As I continue my journey along the America's Haunted Road Trip through North Carolina, the question hits me: How many times during my investigations and travels through North Carolina have I seen a connection between the Civil War and ghost stories? This war created intense trauma and painful memories in this part of the United States. The emotional energy is recorded on the land and in the homes and buildings, keeping the ghosts alive.

New Bern, North Carolina, saw its share of the Civil War. Founded in 1710 near the Trent and Neuse rivers, New Bern was settled by Swiss and German explorers. Their leader was Baron Christoph von Graffenried, and he named the town New Bern after his hometown of Bern, Switzerland. New Bern was an active port in the 1800s and the Union army captured the town during the war in 1862.

The town is loaded with haunted history, with buildings still standing from the 18th century and with more than 150 sites listed on the National Register of Historic Places. New Bern is also the birthplace of Pepsi-Cola, originally named Brad's Drink and created by local pharmacist Caleb Davis Bradham in his drugstore in 1898. Perhaps New Bern's diverse history goes hand in hand with ghosts. It was time to get on the road and find out for myself.

My first destination in New Bern was the Harvey Mansion Historic Inn. The inn was originally a house owned by John Harvey and his family until Union soldiers during the Civil War commandeered the Harvey house and used it as a military headquarters. After the war, the house was used as a dormitory, apartments, and, at one time, a boarding house. The house was almost torn down in 1974 before it was saved and added to the National Register.

In 2003, the Harvey Mansion was restored and renovated. The mansion now operates as an inn, with a restaurant and bar with live entertainment. The inn is inviting and comfortable and takes you back to a time when you might have been traveling to a seaport and required shelter from a friendly innkeeper for the evening. It also has the distinction of being haunted.

The inn continues to generate reports from eyewitnesses who see a woman in their room or in the hallway, only to have her disappear by walking through a wall. Others report seeing a young girl walking around the property. The third floor of the inn was the original living quarters, so if you have the opportunity, spend time in this area, as it might be your best chance to see a ghost.

New Bern is known for its haunted history and has its own Ghosts of New Bern walking ghost tour. The tour covers New Bern's haunted homes, cemeteries, and more. Visit their website at hauntednewbern.com for more information.

At one time, the tour was based on the research of Joseph and Joyce O'Callahan, a husband-and-wife team, who together wrote about the haunted history of New Bern in their book, Ghosts of New Bern. Before he passed, I spoke with Joe O'Callahan about his work as the ghost tour guide to New Bern. His background was in 18th-century literature and history, and he previously worked with the Colonial Williamsburg Foundation, creating a ghost tour there. He and Joyce shared a love of history and hauntings. Joyce grew up in the area and graduated from the University of North Carolina at Chapel Hill. She later worked for the Jamestown Foundation. Their favorite haunted site to visit was the Harvey Mansion, along with the historic downtown and the Isaac Taylor house.

While chatting with locals in the area, several mentioned to me that the Isaac Taylor house is indeed haunted and that Isaac is the great-great-great-great-grandfather of singer James Taylor. Isaac was born in Scotland, and upon moving to the United States, he built a plantation along the Neuse River. Like many plantation owners, he would also build a town house where he would live part of the time. This is the house that stands today. The house was passed down through the family, and during the Civil War, Isaac's granddaughters, Phoebe and Catherine, who were both in their 80s by this time, were living in the house as spinsters. Union soldiers entered the home to take it over, and the two sisters refused to leave. Holding their ground, an agreement was made that the sisters would live on the third floor and the Union troops would live on the first and second floors. A pulley system was created outside the house to lift and lower their food and other supplies to the third floor, and this pulley can still be seen today. The sisters reportedly have never left the house, and their ghosts are still seen and heard in the home, with voices and footsteps heard coming from the third floor. Locals and visitors report seeing apparitions of the sisters standing near the windows of the third floor as they look out onto the street below. Perhaps they still keep watch, hoping that the Union troops never return and they can enjoy their home in peace. The Isaac Taylor house is now private property, and when I visited New Bern, the house was up for sale.

Continuing on my journey, the next place to visit on my list was the Cedar Grove Cemetery, reportedly one of the most haunted cemeteries in the state. Local lore says to be wary of entering the cemetery at night due to the wide variety of restless spirits. It is said if you are pure of heart and come with good intentions you will be safe, but if you come with ulterior motives, the ghosts will come after you.

More than 300 Confederate soldiers were buried here in this cemetery. Reports state that around the year 1900, grave robbers entered the cemetery and broke into most of the graves to steal Civil War memorabilia to sell to collectors. Since that time, residents say that the cemetery has been very active, not from other grave robbers returning for more loot, but rather from the ghosts of the Confederate soldiers who were awoken when their graves were disturbed. They are now active in the cemetery and are in search of their personal memorabilia and jewelry. They now keep watch over the cemetery in order to protect all who rest here.

One of the most fascinating haunting aspects of the cemetery is the Weeping Arch. The arch is used as the opening spot for the parade of ghosts each year during New Bern's October Ghost Walk, but the legend of the arch is much more sinister. I spoke with Joe to confirm the stories that I had heard about the Weeping Arch. According to Joe, the arch is made from a stone called marl, which is a rugged but porous material. When it rains, the Weeping Arch soaks in the rainwater, and then it releases the rain held in the stone for days afterward in slow drips, which leads to the description of the arch weeping.

The legend states that should you walk under the arch and have the arch "weep" on you, you will be the next to die. It's not certain how many times this has actually been the case, but I prefer not to find out firsthand.

The cemetery is both haunted and haunting in its look and feel. Take your camera and a recorder with you, as there's a good chance you'll get orb photos, EVPs, or maybe even a full-body apparition photo.

Joe also shared with me a story about the Christ Church graveyard, which is also believed to be haunted. From 1798 to 1799, a horrific yellow fever epidemic claimed the lives of many of the people of New Bern, devastating the community. People were buried at a fast pace to keep the fever from spreading further. Rapidly running out of room, some people were buried in trenches around the graveyard. It is reported that so many people died and were buried in the Christ Church graveyard that it ran out of space in those two years, which led to the establishment of Cedar Grove Cemetery in 1800.

Local lore states that during that time, some people fell into a coma-like state during the last stages of their illness, leaving them unable to respond or speak. It is believed that in the haste to bury the bodies and make room to treat more people, some of these people were mistakenly thought to be dead and were buried alive. Their ghosts still haunt the graveyard. This story reminded me of the 18- and 19-century custom in Europe and the United States of creating coffins with a cord inside that extended outside up through the ground and was tied to a bell suspended over the grave. Men were hired to work on the "graveyard shift" to listen for ringing bells from those who were mistakenly buried. The "resurrection" of these people gave rise to the popular expression "saved by the bell."

My final stop in the city was the original reason for my visit to New Bern. It was the Attmore-Oliver House, located in a historic district of New Bern. Built in 1790, the house was expanded in 1834. The house is a wonderful example of the unique style of architecture used in North Carolina during this time. The home is painted white with black shutters and has four brick chimneys and generously sized porches on the front and back of the house. The Attmore-Oliver House is best known for two main reasons, one being that it's owned by the New Bern Historical Society and is used for a variety of society functions, and second, that it's the most haunted house in New Bern.

The legend of the haunting begins like this: during the Civil War, Hannah Oliver watched three of her brothers march off to war. Two of her brothers died in battle, while the youngest, George, was injured and returned home. George was 13 years old at the time and had run away from home to join the troops, as he couldn't bear his brothers fighting without him. Through these desperate times of economic hardships, hunger, and loss of her family, Hannah, her husband, William, and their three daughters held on as best they could. Later, after Hannah and her husband passed away, one of their daughters, Mary Oliver, continued to live in the home. Mary took over the family business, which at the time was selling insurance. Mary was born in the home before the Civil War, and she lived in the home for almost a century, passing away in her 90s in 1951.

If seems likely that if anyone were to stay in the home in the afterlife, it would be Mary. It would be the most comfortable place for her to reside. After all, spending almost 100 years in one home has to be some sort of record. Mary's ghost is seen and felt frequently in the home.

Legends state that there are other ghosts in the house, and some believe that there are many of them. Some of the most intense reports of paranormal activity come from the attic. People can be heard walking, moaning, and at times speaking to each other from the attic. Local legend says that a father and daughter were confined in the attic after they had both contracted smallpox. They were reported to have died there, and they continue to haunt the house today. Some reports claim that you can hear the little girl playing with toys and that when people go into the attic, there is a presence there of a protective father who does not wish his daughter to be disturbed. Tours are no longer permitted in the attic at this time, so I wasn't able to travel up there for myself to check things out.

The Attmore-Oliver House is open to the public to tour. One of the displays inside the house is of a doll collection. I have to say I didn't spend much time looking at the collection, as I've had more encounters with dolls having spirits attached to them than I care to reflect upon.

Inside the house is a fascinating look at Victorian, Federal, and Empire furniture, and many of the pieces are original to the family and may hold energy imprints from their lives. It's interesting to take the tour to see if one of the ghosts will appear while you're inside the home, but many locals find it even more eerie when they are walking by at night to see lights and orbs coming from the windows of the attic and the other floors as well, long after the house has been locked up for the evening.

Strange lights and orbs have been seen coming from the windows of the Attmore-Oliver House.

Perhaps Miss Mary roams through her house at night, enjoying her home as she did for almost 100 years, and in the attic, a father still watches over his daughter, wishing he could nurse her back to health.

I didn't experience any paranormal activity while visiting the house, but that's how it goes with ghost hunting; it's all about timing. Spirits, like the living, do what they want to do, when they want to do it. I loved the town of New Bern and plan to visit again soon. Perhaps next time, Miss Mary and I will be able to have a chat.

The beautiful and historic town of Beaufort reports ghostly sightings of Blackbeard and his pirates all around the town.

CHAPTER 10

BEAUFORT

BLACKBEARD THE PIRATE AND THE OLD BURYING GROUNDS

In my journeys throughout North Carolina, I have loved each and every city I have visited. North Carolina has the good fortune to have mountains to the west; rich, fertile lands in the Piedmont; and beautiful beaches on the coast. Because it is so beautiful, more and more people are moving to the state each day, and perhaps for this reason as well, even more people never want to leave the area and so their ghosts continue to stay.

I've seen a lot of haunted hotels, forts, plantations, and cemeteries along my haunted road trip, but rarely have I come across a town with so much "spirit and spirits" as Beaufort, North Carolina.

Beaufort is one of the most inviting coastal areas of the East Coast. Not only do residents agree, but so did Blackbeard the pirate, as he chose to live and die in the area. In 1996, a sunken ship was found in Beaufort Inlet, and as thousands of artifacts continue to be recovered from the wreck, it's looking more positive that this is indeed Blackbeard's ship, the *Queen Anne's Revenge*. These artifacts can be viewed at the North Carolina Maritime Museum in Beaufort.

Blackbeard's wandering ghost is seen often enough along the coast, at times looking for his head, at other times in full form. Perhaps he is seeking to pillage, plunder, and find what many of us are always on the lookout for—a hearty ale.

One thing that we all learn quickly as ghost hunters is that when you want to stir up a ghost, start playing with their belongings, and you'll soon find yourself no longer alone. As protective and attached to the *Queen Anne's Revenge* as Blackbeard became, chances are good that sightings of the pirate will increase as his ship is recovered and eventually displayed in the museum.

When not on his ship, Blackbeard lived part of his life at the Hammock House in New Bern, which in the past has reported a high amount of ghostly activity. According to legend, Blackbeard would anchor his ship and then use a rowboat to row up to the Hammock House. He appeared to enjoy his time in Beaufort and only left town when the British military came looking for him. Their presence forced him to move to a new residence in Bath, North Carolina. Legend states that Blackbeard married many times and that in a fight with his wife at the Hammock House, he flew into a rage and hanged her from an oak tree behind the house.

Witnesses report strange lights floating around the house at night. They say that on some nights, you can still hear the woman screaming in her struggles with Blackbeard as he drags her into the backyard.

Over the years, I've done a lot of research on Blackbeard, and many stories state that as pirates go, he was a fairly peaceful man, preferring to use scare tactics when possible rather than direct conflict. As a lover of history, I know that historic figures can be demonized when falsehoods are written about them. As the old saying goes, "History is written by the victors."

It's no surprise that British captains and officers spread propaganda that greatly exaggerated the pirate's actual deeds. I've seen reports that stated that Blackbeard was quite kind to civilians, especially women. I just don't believe that he hanged a woman from a tree in such a brutal manner, nor did I sense anything of that nature while near the Hammock House. If anything, I would say that if Blackbeard's ghost does appear around the home, it is because he found it to be a peaceful and relaxing place to stay when not on board his ship, and that he continues to enjoy it to this day.

There is no way to confirm that Blackbeard did visit this area, other than from local reports. During my investigations, I heard just as many stories that negated Blackbeard's reputed visits to the Hammock House.

The Hammock House originally served as an inn during Blackbeard's time. The legends state that some of the other guests at the inn may have been crueler than Blackbeard, men such as Richard Russell Jr., whose ghost is also reported to haunt the Hammock House. According to lore, Russell returned from a voyage at sea in 1747 and was in the process of dragging one of his slaves up the stairs to the attic of the Hammock House in order to punish him. The slave fought against Russell along the way and pushed him down the stairs. Russell landed at the bottom of the stairs dead from a broken neck. The story doesn't state what happened to the unfortunate slave, but witnesses report that the ghost of Richard Russell is often heard on the stairs struggling with the slave as he attempts to force him back upstairs.

There's also the story of Captain Madison Brothers, who was engaged to Samantha Ashby of Baltimore. Brothers was known as the jealous type and was always worried about whether Samantha's eye would wander to another man while he was at sea. Brothers was also known for his rash temper, and he soon earned the nickname "Mad." He and Samantha were to be married in Beaufort at the Hammock House. The legend says that she traveled by land with her bridal party to Beaufort, and he traveled by sea on his ship. Along his journey, he experienced several setbacks at sea, including running into a severe storm that broke the ship's mast. Angry at his misfortune, he reportedly began drinking heavily before the ship hit port. The order of what happened next is unclear, though the end of the story is not.

Some reports say that when his ship arrived near Beaufort, the captain boarded a rowboat with some of his crew to head up to the Hammock House to meet up with his fiancée Samantha and attend the engagement party being thrown for them there. As the rowboat neared the bank beside the Hammock House, the Mad captain saw Samantha chatting with another man. This mystery man drew Samantha into his arms and kissed her on the cheek. Outraged by this sight, Mad hit the shore with his sword drawn and challenged the mystery man to a fight. The man had no idea who Mad was and drew his sword to defend himself. The fight was fierce and moved from the backyard into the Hammock House, with the two men slashing away at each other.

Others claim that the legend began as Captain Madison's ship docked in port. As the captain and his crew entered the town of Beaufort, they went for a drink at a local pub before heading over to the captain's engagement party at the Hammock House. While in town at a tavern, the captain overheard idle gossip from the locals wondering who the young man was who had been running all over town the past few days with Madison's fiancée. The locals also went on to tell the captain that this young man was staying at the Hammock House with his fiancée. This news drove an already-drunken Mad into a jealous rage.

Regardless of which way it began, Mad approached the party in the backyard and immediately picked a fight with the man speaking to Samantha. He walked up to his fiancée and yelled, "Betrayed!" And then the fight began. She protested and begged him to listen to her, as did several other people at the party who tried to stop the captain, but his crewmen held them back, saying the fight was a matter of honor.

The captain and the guest fought in the backyard, and the fight then moved into the Hammock House. Inside the house, the mystery man slipped on the stairs, and Mad took this opportunity to use his blade to stab the man deep in the chest, killing him. The captain never even asked the man a single question.

Mad and his crew jumped back in the rowboats at this point and took off to sea in their ship, never to be heard from again. A brokenhearted Samantha was left behind to handle the funeral for the deceased man, as well as to explain to arriving guests that there would be no engagement party or wedding. Who was the man who died so horribly? It was Samantha's brother, Lieutenant Caruthers Ashby. He had traveled to be at his sister's wedding, and he and Captain Mad had not yet met. It is said that there is a bloodstain where he died in the Hammock House that still appears in the home.

Other reports state that Mad later discovered through news that traveled from port to port that he had murdered Samantha's brother, an innocent man—an innocent man who remains to haunt Hammock House to this day. I would imagine that Captain Mad was haunted by this news as well, as he lost his fiancée and his good name to his jealous rage.

One of the most popular haunted stories surrounding the Hammock House ended up providing physical proof of the ghosts that haunt the home. During the Civil War, three Union soldiers were ordered to take control of the Hammock House when Federal forces captured Beaufort. The house was vacant at the time, since many people had left the area before the advancing Union troops. The three officers entered the house, and they were never seen nor heard from again. Almost 60 years later, when renovations were being conducted near the back porch, workman uncovered the skeletal remains of the three soldiers. Many locals claim to see the ghosts of these soldiers walking around the Hammock House, still searching the grounds.

With so much death surrounding the house, the likelihood of seeing orbs or ghosts in the windows of the house or on the grounds is high.

The Hammock House has reportedly had more than 31 owners and is now private property. Trespassing is not permitted. There is a local ghost tour in Beaufort, though, that will take you past the home and tell you the full story during the tour. I drove past the home and have to say psychically I felt more residual anger from the neighbors who perhaps are weary of ghost hunters wandering around their neighborhood.

One of my destinations in Beaufort was the Old Burying Ground Cemetery. It has been preserved and taken care of by the town and the Beaufort Historic Association. The cemetery has a genteel beauty to it, and the grounds are peaceful looking, with ancient oak trees and vines growing all around. It also has an active history of ghostly appearances. This cemetery has some of the most unusual gravesites I have ever seen—and I've seen plenty.

The Old Burying Ground Cemetery is the final resting place of soldiers from the War of 1812, the Revolutionary War, and the Civil War. Locals report frequent sightings of soldiers walking the grounds at nightfall.

Some of the earliest graves were simply covered with slabs of cypress, others with seashells. A man identified as Captain Burns is buried here with a cannon from his ship on top of his gravestone, and a soldier is reportedly buried here standing straight up so that he could salute his king, even in death, while others disagree and claim that this gravesite is the final resting place of Lieutenant Caruthers Ashby, Samantha's brother who died in the Hammock House.

One unusual grave is that of a little girl who was buried in a rum keg. She died at sea, and the captain placed her small body in a rum keg until the ship could land in Beaufort to give her a proper burial. Local children and adults visit her gravesite in the cemetery often and cover her grave with toys and flowers.

My experience tells me that the cemetery is haunted, it's active, and if you want to experience seeing a ghost or sensing paranormal activity, this is a good place to do it. If you are psychic or sensitive at all, you will sense the presence of spirits as you near the area. Having said that, I also want to add that it is one of the most well-cared-for cemeteries that I have ever seen, so if you decide to take a trip and visit the Old Burying Ground, please be kind, considerate, and respectful. Tread lightly and have respect for the people who are buried there, as this area has been their resting place for hundreds of years. As well, respect the local people who have worked diligently over the years to care for, protect, and preserve this state treasure.

When planning a trip to Beaufort for ghost hunting, you'll find a wonderful variety of places to explore. It's also close to Fort Macon, which I've discussed earlier in the book, so you can easily see both on the same weekend, if desired.

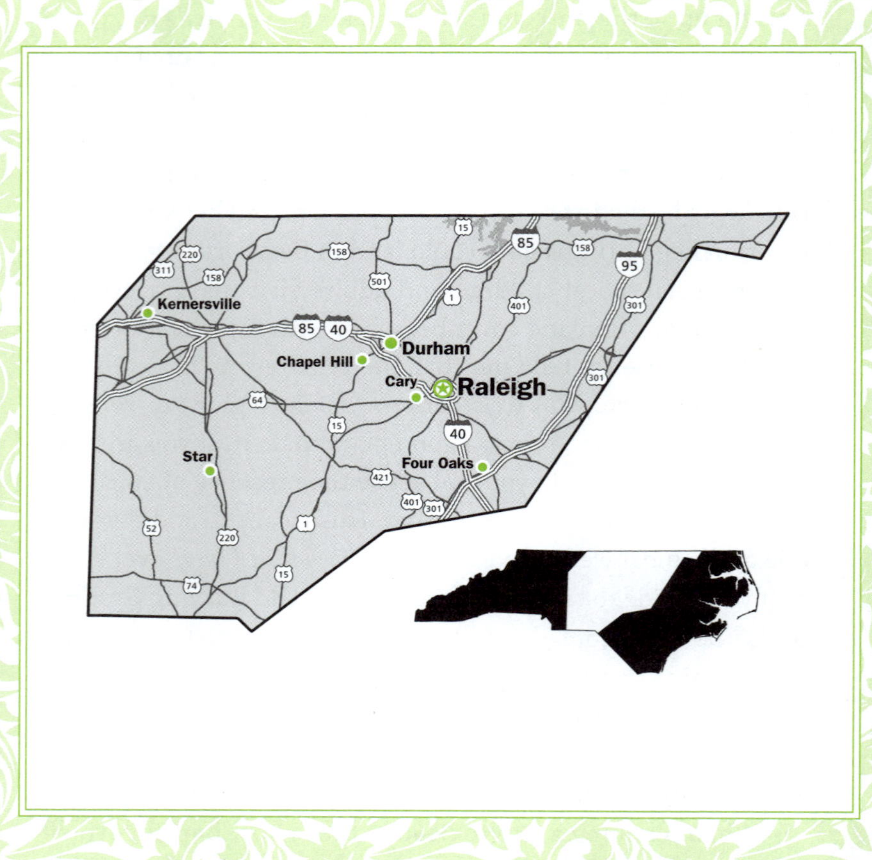
Kernersville
Durham
Chapel Hill
Cary
Raleigh
Star
Four Oaks

CENTRAL CAROLINA

THE PIEDMONT, THE TRIANGLE, AND THE TRIAD

The Star Hotel is located in the geographical center of the state.
(Photo by Gary Spivey)

CHAPTER 11

STAR

MISS DEBORAH STILL LOOKS AFTER YOU AT THE STAR HOTEL

Star is known as the geographical center of North Carolina and once served as the junction where the East/West railway met the North/South railway. In 1866, gold was discovered in the area; by 1874, gold mining was in full operation. According to the last reported census information, the town of Star consists of 1.2 miles and has fewer than 1,000 residents.

In 1896, Star was growing as a town, shipping lumber, turpentine, and bricks on the railroads. Traffic was increasing in Star, and a large wooden hotel known as the Star Hotel Bed & Breakfast was built to accommodate passengers traveling through the area. Passengers disembarked from the trains and stayed at the Star Hotel before catching another train the next morning.

A lot has changed in the town over the years. Currently, Star is known for its proximity to the town of Seagrove, where the state's most talented artisans create pottery and art. Over the years, the Star Hotel fell upon hard times, and its future looked so bleak that people thought the hotel might not stand much longer. This would have been the case had it not been for Gary Spivey. You may know Gary for his wild white hair and his work as one of America's most popular psychics. I was able to sit down and chat with him about his hometown of Star and to ask him about the haunted activity of the Star Hotel. It's quite a story.

In 2004, Gary was visiting Star. He had spent time in the company of family and friends and was heading back out of town when he passed the dilapidated Star Hotel. As he drove by, he heard a voice tell him to buy the hotel. Gary, a world-renowned psychic who performs in Las Vegas and around the world, is used to hearing the voices of his spirit guides and angels prompting him when to take action in certain situations.

Gary was on a tight schedule and didn't have time to stop and look at the hotel, so he argued with his guides, telling them that he must have misunderstood; what would he do with a hotel in Star, North Carolina? They persisted that he needed to purchase the property, so he picked up his phone and called his sister, who lives in Star, and asked her to go tour the property. She checked out the place and said it was in poor shape but that it was a beautiful and historic place with good bones. Gary made an offer and bought the hotel without ever stepping foot on the premises.

Once he purchased the hotel, Gary and one of his business partners went to check out the property. They stayed in the hotel overnight. Gary describes it as feeling creepy inside, and both men had a restless night's sleep, each reporting from their rooms a feeling of someone watching them as they tossed and turned.

Gary began reconstruction on the hotel, and strange reports began to trickle in from construction workers on the site. Some would hear a baby crying in one of the rooms, and another saw a ghost of a man who reportedly fell off the roof and died when the hotel was originally being constructed. At night, while Gary slept in the hotel, a lady began to appear to him in the room. She had long black hair and was dressed conservatively from an older time. One night as she visited him, she said, "I'm really happy with what you are doing with my hotel." She never identified herself to Gary, so he was unsure of who she was, even as she continued to visit.

A ghost named Deborah is a permanent resident of the Star Hotel. The Deborah Leach suite is named after her and she is often seen in the suite and around the hotel. *(Photo by Gary Spivey)*

One day, Gary discovered photos of the hotel from its earliest days. While looking through the photos, Gary recognized the woman who visited him in the evenings. It was Deborah Leach, the wife of Angus Leach. The Leaches were the original owners of the Star Hotel and ran the hotel during its peak when the railroad brought passengers through the area each day.

As the construction progressed on the hotel, Deborah began to appear on a regular basis. Today, Deborah often makes her presence known to the staff and guests throughout the hotel. When she appears, she is busy working in the bedrooms, in the kitchen, or in the dining room. Everyone who reports seeing her ghost finds her to be welcoming, and she appears to be happy with the hotel in operation again.

The Star Hotel is the largest Queen Anne structure built in central North Carolina. Built in 1896, she's quite striking, with a rounded front porch that wraps around the building. As you enter the hotel, the first thing you'll notice is the grand staircase, which was built by the Cooper brothers. The Cooper brothers were master craftsmen who are best known for having built the grand staircase for the *Titanic*. The hotel is full of Victorian antiques and beautifully renovated with fireplaces and woodwork original to the hotel.

When renovating the Star Hotel, Gary wanted to honor the people who had owned and cared for it over the years, so he named the suites after each of the four owners. The suite named for Deborah Leach is the bedroom where she most often appears. Visitors report seeing her ghost appear to them in the room, as well as in other parts of the hotel. Guests share stories of seeing her in their dreams, while others see her appearing before them as she welcomes them to the hotel.

One of the suites is named for current owner Gary Spivey. He's decorated his suite with giant healing crystals, along with beautiful antiques and works of art.

Gary continued to wonder why his spirit guides and angels were so adamant about him buying the hotel in Star and renovating the property. As he was researching the history of the hotel and the gold mining history of the area, he discovered something quite interesting. Along with the gold in the area, there is an overwhelming amount of white quartz crystal in the soil. Quartz crystals hold energy, and whatever energy is put into the crystals radiates out with stronger energy. Gary then realized that the positive energy he was putting back into the hotel and on the land would be stored in the white quartz crystals, which would expand and radiate outward into the area.

Gary was then led to plant a rose garden on the property and to build a 17-foot-tall water fountain. His guides led him to pick the right location and were helpful in each step of the process. Once the fountain was in place and the garden complete, Gary felt the energy shift on the property. He was then able to see a vortex opening between the higher spiritual planes and the earth plane in this location. During this time, Gary's guides and angels showed him that there are areas all around the world where the energy can connect between the two planes. When they are opened and filled with positive energy, wonderful things can happen at these locations. Gary immediately began to feel the change in the energy on the land and was excited to see what the results would provide.

He didn't have to wait long. Guests began reporting that while visiting the rose garden and fountain, the most wondrous things were happening to them. Many reported that while spending time in the garden, angels began to appear to them. Others reported that their deceased relatives had appeared to them in the garden to share messages of love with them. Several reported receiving spiritual gifts and blessings while in the garden.

Gary reports that the energy continues to grow and expand in the garden and that the vortex connects from the higher planes directly into the water fountain, mixing with the water. He's beginning to understand some of the reasons that he is meant to be in North Carolina.

I couldn't help but reflect upon this information, thinking that with Star being in the geographic center of North Carolina, should enough positive energy begin to resonate from this vortex, it could radiate and stimulate a very positive effect of energy throughout the entire state.

I shared with Gary my story of how my husband and I had decided one day that it was time for us to move from where we were living in Florida. My husband and I held hands and asked our guides to show us a sign of where to go, if it was for our highest and best purpose that we were meant to move. The next day, my husband was at work when a recruiter called out of the blue and offered him a job. My husband was familiar with the company, as he had worked for this company previously in Florida. The recruiter told him that the job was not in Florida, but rather in North Carolina. He offered to fly us both up there for my husband to interview for the job and to see the area. Neither one of us had ever been to North Carolina and had never considered moving there, but we agreed to travel to North Carolina for the interview.

We were in a hotel in Research Triangle Park, and to be honest, I was having a difficult time with the energy in the area. It felt closed, tight, and a little dark. Where I was living in Florida was on the Gulf shores with a lot of peaceful spiritual energy floating around. We sat in the hotel talking before it was time for his interview, and we decided that this wasn't the place for us to move. We wondered how to get out of the situation.

Like Gary, I'm a psychic, and I've always relied on assistance from my guides to show me what to do; also like Gary, I argue with them from time to time when they suggest things that don't make sense to me. I knew they were responsible for getting us here to this interview, but I couldn't understand why they would want us to move here. So I suggested to my husband that we ask that the company double his salary and agree to pay for our move to North Carolina, including shipping our vehicles and offering some assistance in purchasing a house in the area. We talked it over, and I thought this way my husband could do his best in the interview as he always does, but the terms would just be too high, so they would decline to offer him the job. He went to the interview, came back to the hotel, and we returned home, thinking it was over and wondering what in the world our guides had been thinking.

Forty-eight hours later, the recruiter called with the news that the company was offering my husband the job and had agreed to all of our terms. A moving company was on its way to pack up our house and move us to North Carolina. To say we were shocked would be an understatement. It was then that we both realized that our guides had a definitive reason and purpose for us to move to North Carolina, and while we were unsure of the reason why, we couldn't argue with the fact that it appeared to be our destiny.

Sharing this story with Gary, I explained that I believe North Carolina is going to be a very important place in holding positive energy for this part of the world as we go through our next evolution on a body, mind, spirit, and planetary level. I believe that North Carolina is evolving into a light center for the United States. I see the symbolism with the lighthouses all along the North Carolina coast, shining brightly. They remind me of the great lighthouse in Alexandria, Egypt, where the world's greatest library once existed. On the other end of the state lie the mystical Blue Ridge Mountains, one of the oldest mountain ranges in the world, and with vortices in the area spinning with so much energy in cities like Asheville that the area has been nicknamed the Sedona of the South, in reference to the vortices and spiritual energy in Sedona, Arizona.

I believe that Gary Spivey has returned here to stimulate this energy in Star, North Carolina. As the energy is raised in the geographical center of the state, it will radiate outward throughout the state. Gary has strengthened his commitment to Star, purchasing other buildings along Main Street in the town and renovating them. The new tenants include artists, musicians, and shop owners.

Inside the Star Hotel, the energy is warm and inviting. As a person who sees auras, I can see the energy not just around people but also around buildings, plants, and animals. While tapping into the energy around the fountain, I could see symbols in the energy coming from around the water. Some of these symbols I recognize from ancient teachings, and there is a very powerful energy around the area. People report feeling their bodies heating up and their energy levels rising while in the garden. Gary has begun offering spiritual workshops at the hotel, and they have been very well received. The hotel is vibrating with positive energy, and I believe that the town is in the process of evolving into a spiritual center that will grow in magnitude over the years.

When visiting the Star Hotel, keep your eye out for Deborah Leach, who will enjoy welcoming you. But even more importantly, relax, take a deep breath, and spend some time in the garden with the fountain, where you just might have a deeply personal spiritual experience, such as a meeting with a loved one from the other side or one of your angels or guides. You may also wish to bring a piece of quartz crystal with you so that you can store the energy of your time spent in the garden and have it with you always.

DEVIL'S TRAMPING GROUND, CHATHAM COUNTY

For the past 300 years, residents and visitors to Chatham County have discussed the anomaly known in the area as the Devil's Tramping Ground. Located about 10 miles west of Siler City in the woods, the tramping ground is a circle measuring 40 feet in diameter in which nothing ever grows. Trees and a wide variety of vegetation surround the area, but the circle itself remains clear and empty. Nothing ever grows inside the Devil's Tramping Ground.

Local legend says that the ground looks this way because the devil uses this plot of land to pace in a circle, walking round and round as he plans new ways to spread more evil on earth. If the design was more elaborate, perhaps it would have been called the Devil's Labyrinth, but in this case, it remains in its original circle form.

Interestingly, during my research in North Carolina, I found that many areas across the state are named for the devil. Duke University in Durham has the Blue Devils for their school mascot, and a city along the coast of North Carolina is named Kill Devil Hills. In Cary, North Carolina, Cary High School was the first public high school built in North Carolina in 1896. Their school mascot is the Imps. Imps are small mischievous demons from German folklore. They are known to be wild and uncontrollable, fond of pranks and misleading people. Imps can be contained or bound in enchanted objects. What a fascinating name to give to a high school mascot.

Could it be that some sinister being has been roaming the state of North Carolina for centuries, and does it do its daily planning in the Devil's Tramping Ground?

There are hundreds of stories about people who have been to the Devil's Tramping Ground and attempted to camp there overnight. They

report waking up to find themselves and all of their gear removed from the circle. Others report tossing rocks, branches, bottles, and other items into the circle, only to find them removed from the circle a short while later.

Not everyone believes that the anomaly is connected to the devil. In the 1700s, settlers in the area believed that it was a sacred area belonging to the Native American tribes that used to live there. The tribes reportedly held ceremonies and rituals in the area, and it is said that the land stills holds the magic and energy created there by the tribe.

Several scientific groups have conducted testing on the soil in the circle, and it contains a high level of salt and acidity. None of the studies or theories have explained why the soil would contain these items in such elevated levels. Even more peculiar, the soil outside of the circle tests as normal. There is also no explanation as to why the area remains a perfect circle, empty of all vegetation to this day.

Referred to as one of the strangest houses in the world, Korner's Folly was designed by Jule Korner, an interior designer who used each room to showcase his work.

CHAPTER 12

KERNERSVILLE

VISIT WITH THE GUARDIAN OF KORNER'S FOLLY

Located in the peaceful landscape of the Piedmont area of North Carolina lies the town of Kernersville in the area known as the Triad. The Triad consists of three major cities: Greensboro, Winston-Salem, and High Point. Kernersville is a beautiful small town that is actively restoring and renovating its historic downtown area. I enjoyed my time there, exploring the historic area and seeing beautiful homes lovingly cared for, such as the Harmon House.

The locals invited me to return in the spring to enjoy their largest citywide event called Spring Folly, a live music event. In the spring, the town also hosts a Victorian Ball, which guests attend in traditional Victorian-period attire, including ball gowns, tuxedos, and military uniforms from the era. Both of these events have a connection to one of the most interesting architectural achievements in Kernersville. It may also be one of the strangest homes in the world, built in 1880. It's called Korner's Folly, and if I had to compare it to other strange homes, I would say that it is a miniature version of the Winchester Mystery House in San Jose, California. It also shares another similarity with the Winchester House, as they're both reported to be haunted.

The original owner of Korner's Folly was Jule Gilmer Korner. He named the home Korner's Folly when a cousin, or possibly a neighbor, declared the home to be just that. Korner was so amused by the comment that he made it the official name of the home, even going so far as to hang a plaque with that name outside the house. Korner was a painter and interior designer and is best known for painting signs for the Bull Durham Bulls across the South.

Unlike the Winchester Mystery Mansion, Korner's Folly was deliberately designed with style in mind. At the Winchester House, Sarah Winchester, upon the advice of a psychic, had carpenters build new rooms in her house 24 hours a day until her death. Sarah Winchester was the heir to the Winchester rifle fortune, and the psychic had told her that she and her family were haunted by angry spirits that had been killed by Winchester rifles and wanted to punish the family. This ongoing construction was supposed to confuse and trick the angry spirits and keep them from locating Sarah Winchester in her home and haunting her. Inside the home, doors can open to several-story drops below, and staircases lead to the ceiling, going nowhere. The entire house winds around like a maze, and by the time you've walked through it, you've walked more than a mile. The effect is eerie, confusing, and at times maddening. While Korner's Folly also has a variety of unique rooms and twists and turns, the effect feels very different; it's charming, and each room pulls you into an experience for the senses.

Korner created Korner's Folly for an entirely different reason, and ghosts were the furthest things from his mind. A talented artist, Korner wanted the house to be a showplace for his work, both artistically in size and scale, in order to give prospective clients an idea of the various types of interior design that he could create in their homes and buildings. The house has 22 rooms, and there's no easy way to describe them. Each room is unique; some are fit for royalty and are palatial in scale. There are trap doors, more than 15 different styles of fireplaces, cubbyholes to tuck away in, murals, and a library.

Whimsical touches are all around Korner's Folly, including this adorable Witch's Corner.

I love Korner's Folly. It reminds me of playing dress up when I was young; how one day I wanted to be a princess, another day the queen, and I'd rotate from the Victorian Era, to the Roaring Twenties, to holding court in the Middle Ages. Living in Korner's Folly would have been like living in a dollhouse. How much fun the children must have had growing up here! While I was immediately entranced by the whimsical parts of the home, I must also say that it has elegant touches: murals, a striking reception room, and a wonderful little theater named Cupid's Park. Korner's Folly grabbed me at the front door; it's simply enchanting. It should be no surprise that the home is on the National Register of Historic Places.

Even the exterior of Korner's Folly grabs my attention instantly. It looks like no other home I have seen throughout all of North Carolina. If I had to place the home in an area where it would fit in with other architectural styles, I might say that it would look best as a cottage on the Biltmore estate in Asheville.

None of the 22 rooms look the same in any way. There are three floors and seven levels to the home, some with ceilings as low as 6 feet while other ceilings reach heights of more than 25 feet. Hallways have different sizes; some are quite narrow, and the effect can be striking as you follow a passageway into a new room, some with doorways over 10 feet tall. Extensively detailed woodwork is displayed in every room. A winding staircase takes you from floor to floor, and on the fourth floor is the first private children's little theater in the United States. The effect of it all is stunning. Jule Korner was definitely talented and had a wonderful artistic eye. The architecture and antique furniture that he designed are visible throughout the home. Korner was also a painter, and his artwork is on display.

Legend says that Korner did not originally plan to live in the home full-time; he built it to display his substantial skills as an artist and designer and intended to use it as his office. During this time, he fell in love with and married Polly Alice Masten. His wife loved the home, and they decided to live in it full time. Over the years, Korner continued to design parts of the home, including creating a unique air distribution system that seems to operate from a series of openings covered with grates in the floors of the home. When the grates are opened, cool air flows from beneath the house and circulates through the rooms through a unique set of windows that pivot according to the airflow.

I spoke with Bruce Frankel, the director of Korner's Folly, to find out more about how Korner had designed and constructed the home and to discuss the haunted activity there. For several years now, Bruce has allowed paranormal investigators to conduct research in the house. Each time a team investigates Korner's Folly, researchers and witnesses report paranormal activity in the home. Some of the best evidence recorded, according to Frankel, was by an area group affiliated with The Atlantic Paranormal Society (TAPS) that conducted an investigation in 2009. During this investigation, they recorded EVPs (Electronic Voice Phenomena) in which a little girl is heard talking and playing in the home, saying things such as "peekaboo." Video recorders also captured a light source floating in the air, which followed people on the video as they walked from room to room.

The center of most of the activity seems to be Cupid's Park Theater, a Shakespearean-style theater decorated with cherubs prancing around on the walls. The room was originally designed as a dance room and billiards parlor. In later renovations it became an art studio for Korner, and then in 1896, his wife turned it into a children's theater, which was used by all the children in the community. Here in this room and in the children's playroom is where most of the haunted activity occurs.

More than 75% of the furniture in the home is original to the house. Science has explained to us that all matter is energy, and with hauntings, we often see land and homes that hold the emotional energy of the occupants who lived in a home for a long period of time. We can "feel" a sad house or a happy home and sense the energy in a building or on the land. When something very unsettling and negative occurs, such as a battle, the emotional energy of this event stays on the land for a long time. Likewise, when a family has lived in a home for many years where children played and great joy and love were radiated for years, it can be felt as well. When energy, negative or positive, is expressed in one area for a long period of time, it leaves an energy imprint, just like the haunted imprints that I've discussed here in this book. Furniture, like other objects, can hold the emotional energy of the home. With so much of the furniture in Korner's Folly being original to the home, the energy of the family is felt throughout the rooms and around the property. As well, and further leading to the strong presence of the family, Korner personally designed and created every room with great intention, passion, and focus, placing even more energy into every inch of the space. Whether it remains a museum or if it becomes a private home, the occupants and visitors will always be in the shadow of his ghost, simply because of the large amount of creative energy placed into building and designing this unique home.

The ghosts reported in Korner's Folly are childlike, playful, and friendly. They appear to be a mix of both energy-imprint hauntings along with one or two interactive playful ghosts. Perhaps Korner himself stayed behind to enjoy the home that he was forever changing and redesigning.

The house was always a work in process, with both Korner and the staff at Korner's Folly, who continue to find decorative surprises during renovations and restorations. One of the most recent discoveries was that while removing wallpaper from the wall near the stairs, they found small drawings underneath that Korner had once hand-painted all the way along the staircase.

Folly Director Frankel reports having changed his opinion of ghosts and the afterlife after working at Korner's Folly. He's personally felt areas in the home that have cold spots, where one side of your body will feel completely chilled while the other side remains at room temperature. He's an advocate of encouraging research into the supernatural and enjoys having paranormal researchers at the home to investigate.

The Korners loved children. They had two, Gilmer and Dore, and Mrs. Korner brought in a music teacher and bought instruments for any children who wished to learn how to play. She organized musical programs in the home with the local children, and parents and the local community were invited to attend the performances.

Research conducted by several paranormal groups has reported EVP recordings in the children's room, the sewing room, the theater, and even in the outhouse. Many times it's the sound of laugher coming from children at play, perhaps time-loop recordings of the years when so many children filled the home to learn about music and play with the Korner children.

Jule Korner died in 1924, and Polly passed on in 1934. It is said that Korner remarked before his passing that he felt he had not finished the work that he had wanted to do on the house. Many feel his spirit in the home and believe that he remains there as its caretaker and guardian.

The home has been wonderfully preserved. Several locals in the area told me that the house once served as an antiques store and also a funeral home in the past. "*Ring, ring,*" says my warning bell! What a perfect combination to create a haunted building! Antiques carry the emotional energies of their owners, and grief is thick in a funeral home, where the dead come to attend their own funeral; together, it's a psychic's perfect storm.

Korner's Folly appeared to me to contain the energy of playfulness and whimsy. One of the most delightful things that I discovered during my time there was that the former director of Korner's Folly, Connie Martin, has always loved the home. As a native of Kernersville, she had a strong desire to help make the Korner's Folly home well known nationally and to continue the work to preserve and care for the home.

A prime example of discovering what you love and then following that passion, Connie worked as the Director of Korner's Folly for six years. Along the way, true love sneaked in and found her in a unique way. Her story is the story that we read about in fairy tales, which only further confirms my hunch that Korner's Folly in an enchanted place.

As the director of the home, Connie met Jule Korner IV, the great-grandson of Jule Korner, and they fell in love. She resigned as the director in order to marry and begin her new life with Mr. Korner IV. When hearing the story, it's easy to feel that Korner may be hanging around the home playing Cupid, which synchronistically is the name of the children's theater in the home. Perhaps he saw the love Connie Martin had for his home and then worked his magic to bring her into the family.

The spirits are very active at the house, and paranormal investigators continue to find evidence of ghostly activity. While I visited Korner's Folly, it was decorated for the Christmas holidays. I felt ghostly activity and energy around the Christmas decorations and detected them moving slightly back and forth on several occasions. Perhaps the ghost children were at play, looking to see if Christmas presents would soon be on display for them. During your visit to Korner's Folly, expect to be charmed and enchanted by the beauty, the whimsy, and the playful spirits.

WHISPERS FROM BEYOND THE GRAVE AT CABE'S LAND CEMETERY

About 6 miles north of downtown Durham, the Eno River and the West Point Mill can be found; they are part of the Eno River State Park. This area was once the home of the Occaneechi, Shakori, and Eno Native American tribes, and the park now consists of 3,900 acres and expands into Durham and Orange counties. In the 1700s, farmers and millers arrived in the area and built the West Point Mill. Each year the Festival for the Eno is held here, and it typically brings 30,000 visitors to the river for three days.

Located in the park is Cabe's Land Trail, a 2-mile walking trail that is rated moderately difficult for hikers. There are three things that always catch the attention of hikers along this trail—a large variety of mushrooms growing along the trail, the old Eno Quarry filled with ground water (where people often swim even though posted signs warn people of submerged trees and equipment in the quarry), and the long-abandoned Cabe's Land Cemetery.

Hikers have long reported paranormal activity as they near the cemetery, located about 200 yards off the main trail. Most interesting about their reports is that the majority of witnesses hear the ghosts talking rather than see apparitions of the ghosts. Paranormal researchers and investigators visit the area in order to capture EVPs (electronic voice phenomena) of the ghostly conversations, and many have reported success with their endeavors, as well as hearing the ghostly voices themselves. (EVPs are recordings that capture voices that are not heard at the time by the human ear but are caught on the recorder.)

WHISPERS FROM BEYOND THE GRAVE AT CABE'S LAND CEMETERY (CONTINUED)

Digital photos have been taken at the same time that the voices were heard in the area, but there are currently no reports from anyone having captured any of the ghostly figures on film.

The cemetery is believed to have been the family cemetery of John Cabe and was established in 1808. Records state that there are 12 marked graves and 39 unmarked graves. It doesn't appear to make a difference what time of day or night or season hikers approach the cemetery; the ghosts reportedly speak to each other at all hours.

CHAPTER 13

DURHAM

GHOSTS FUEL THE FIRE AT STAGVILLE PLANTATION

The land surrounding Stagville appears to be haunted by several ghosts and entities. In 1860, the family owned 30,000 acres and almost 900 slaves.

Outside of Durham lies the plantation of Stagville, which once comprised several thousand acres in the center of land owned by the Bennehan-Cameron families. These two families once owned 30,000 acres in the area, and almost 900 slaves worked on the property, making their enormous estate one of the largest in North Carolina.

After the Civil War, the extensive acreage was broken

up and divided into many parts. The area of Stagville now consists of 71 acres, which are separated into three land tracts. What is most distinctive about the Stagville Plantation is that both the Bennehan and the Cameron families documented all the workings of their life on the plantation throughout the years. These collections of papers were donated to the North Carolina State Archives and the Southern Historical Collection at the University of North Carolina at Chapel Hill. These written accounts have allowed the caretakers of Stagville to provide some of the most detailed accounts of plantation life in North Carolina and the history surrounding the land. Along with the documented history, which is rare to find from that time, I also discovered that Stagville has more standing structures than other plantation homes I have visited throughout the state. There are several plantations that have reconstructed slave quarters and other structures, but the buildings at Stagville are the originals.

Structures still standing include the Bennehan plantation home, built in the late 18th century; four two-story slave family dwellings; a pre–Revolutionary War yeoman farmer's home; a massive timber-framed barn, which is referred to as the Great Barn; and the Bennehan Cemetery, located a short walk just southeast of the Bennehan home.

Over time, nature has had its way with the manmade structures at Stagville. The landscape changes and things decay, but some remnants remain of how the plantation grounds originally looked, including the foundations of several slave dwellings and other buildings that were used for various types of work.

While researching the plantation, I found that it still maintains the Osage orange trees and other plantings, which were popular during the operation of the plantation. Osage orange trees have a wonderful scent in the summer when the oranges are ripe. For most people, scent is a powerful memory trigger that can bring a person back in time to a particular memory. I can smell honeysuckle and I'm immediately transported to my childhood in Louisiana, smelling honeysuckle on the vine. Knowing how powerful scent is for human beings, I have to wonder if the presence of trees and other plantings that harken back to certain times and spaces would also have a similar effect on the ghosts on the property.

What's fascinating about the Osage orange trees is that, at first glance, you'd think they were just another type of orange tree. Big deal, right? They're actually quite amazing and, yes, while they do produce oranges, you probably wouldn't want to eat them. The oranges are a little shriveled in shape, and inside there are hundreds of seeds and the fruit is tough and has a stringy texture. Why then would plantation owners plant so many fruit trees that would produce fruit that only squirrels would enjoy eating? The answer is quite fascinating. The Osage orange trees are planted side by side to create fences. They have thorns, and their wood is extremely strong. When planted close together, they create a structure that is very secure, and the thorns add an additional reinforcement that rivals barbed wire. It's said these trees could be used for fencing to keep horses and hogs inside their pens, as well as keeping wild animals from venturing around the livestock and home while protecting them from high wind and storms. These amazing trees are termite-resistant and were used by Native American tribes to make bows and other useful tools. In addition, the wood from Osage orange trees is used to make magic wands, as their energy is reported to be very powerful when used to connect with earth energy for magical purposes.

While touring the grounds, you're surrounded by trees, so you have to use your imagination to picture how the landscape used to appear. The land was once cleared with large open fields, and according to documentation, there were many more buildings on the land than what currently stands.

Historians and archaeologists continue to research the area to uncover the buried past. An unmarked gravesite has been found that may have been the burial ground of earlier settlers. The skulls found in this area show signs that tomahawks may have crushed them. This evidence, along with other documentation found on site, has led scholars to believe that Native Americans also lived on the land now called Stagville before the plantation was built there. So, both a cemetery and sacred Native American burial ground may have been disturbed during the building of Stagville.

Furthermore, the area holds the emotional energy of the enslaved people who worked the land and many who died there, as well as energy from Civil War activity, all of which make the plantation a good place for paranormal investigations. It's important to conduct due diligence and research when ghost hunting so that you have an idea of what era the ghosts came from, as this can make it easier to communicate with them.

Many haunted sites have more than one ghost, and these ghosts could be from various generations and not connected to each other. For example, at Stagville, you could have Native American ghosts, early colonist ghosts, Civil War ghosts, and slave ghosts all haunting this same area. These ghosts may or may not interact with each other. If the ghost is Native American with a native name, he's probably not going to respond to someone walking around asking if Mr. Joe is in the house. If the ghost is a small child, it may not speak up when someone is walking around asking if Mr. Smith is willing to speak to him or her.

Many times during an investigation, it's better to go in without expectations and just get a feel for the lay of the house and the land. If the ghost wants to be seen or heard, it will make its presence known soon enough.

In the large family graveyard at Stagville, it is surprising to find that there are only three gravesites, those of Richard,

Mary, and Thomas Bennehan. The welcome center at Stagville provides copies of the inscriptions written on the tombstones if you are interested in reading them. They are too worn to read directly from the stones. I found this quite interesting, and during my chat with some people there who were also interested in the inscriptions, I learned that many people bring paper to cemeteries and collect rubbings of stone markers and display them as artwork.

Surrounding the gravesites, there is a wall made of stone with its original iron gate still standing.

The Bennehan's daughter Rebecca married Duncan Cameron and moved to Fairntosh; she and her family are buried in Hillsborough. The Bennehan's son Thomas, who is buried at the family gravesite, never married or had children.

What remains a mystery is where the plantation slaves who died were buried, as there are always some deaths over time and with 900 people, there were certainly more than a few. The burial grounds have not been found, and some speculate that they may have been further out on the property, which is now privately owned. Due to the tremendous amount of documents provided by the family about the workings of the plantation, I found it surprising that these deaths and burials sites were not listed or recorded within the documents.

Several artifacts along with documentation provide some of the best views that I've found into the lives of enslaved people in North Carolina. The reports state that many of the people were skilled craftsmen and artisans and that they were second generation, being American born, rather than having been stolen directly from Africa.

Beyond the documentation, the land itself is well-preserved and has remained intact, so the energy is strong and radiates around the area. As I walked around the plantation, I would occasionally touch the side of a building or other physical objects, using psychometry (a form of ESP where as you touch or hold an object, the energy held in the object tells you about its history). Everywhere I went, I worked to pick up on the energy of the land and the spirits that inhabit it.

In 1980, during restoration of the property, two divining sticks were found inside the wall of one of the slave quarters. Divining sticks were used to find water and other elemental sources under the land. They were also hung in homes to bring protection and attract good and helpful spirits. Some call them dowsing rods, as they are used as a form of divination called dowsing. They've been used by many cultures for thousands of years. They only fell out of favor during the Dark Ages in Europe, when they were labeled as evil and the name was changed to "water witching." I was unable to confirm if these divining sticks were made from the Osage orange trees on the property, but I'd be willing to bet that they were.

Dowsing later became popular again, basically because it produced results. When you're looking to move to a strange land and you need to find a water source quickly so that you, your family, and your livestock will survive, you've only got limited time and resources to find underground water. Dowsers have a good record of results, and people will tend to look the other way if the process used is something that they need.

I've used divining/dowsing rods made from wood and from copper and have had good results with them. They can be used to locate water, oil, metals, gemstones, and even bones from unmarked gravesites. I was first introduced to using them while I lived in Texas. Some oil companies have been known to hire dowsers to help find oil when the wells have run dry and they have exhausted other efforts. Dowsing rods can also be useful tools when used by an intuitive person to detect vortices of energy and ley lines. Ley lines are magnetic currents of energy running coherently along the earth. The aligned energy of ley lines can be detected by dowsing. Ancient monuments, sacred sites, and underground water springs are often found along these lines.

Cowrie seashells, which are an important part of West African religious traditions, were also found around these quarters. They are a representation of the goddess/divine feminine energy and are also a symbol of protection. Cowrie shells are typically placed on a window and around the home on doorknobs, or strung into necklaces and bracelets to wear around the body.

So, here I am at one of the largest plantation sites in North Carolina. I know some of the history, I've got a good idea of the layout of the home and the land, and there are plenty of structures to check out, as well as the cemetery and the surrounding grounds. Let's go ghost hunting!

I have to say that I researched the area well before beginning to tune in intuitively, and I spoke with guides and locals who are familiar with the area. I don't usually do this, as I prefer to go in cold for a reading and then research afterward to see if what I saw and felt can be matched to records. In this case though, I was working in reverse. I knew what others had seen and now I wanted to see if I could see it for myself.

The reports of Stagville being haunted go back more than 100 years, and I've spoken with several other paranormal research teams that have investigated the area. They all agree that it is haunted. Locals and neighbors continually report disturbances on the property, such as hearing shrill screams at night. They also report seeing strange lights floating all around the property, especially near the slave quarters. Some witnesses, including people who have worked on the grounds as caretakers and landscapers, have seen a young African American girl appear before them as they worked. Her sudden appearance has scared many of them enough to leave the area. She appears to be wandering around looking for her father, and has reportedly asked several people if they would help her find him.

I was also told by several people that the sheriff's department and the fire department have both been called several times to the property to investigate reports of African American men near the Great Barn at sunset. There have also reportedly been several false alarms of the Great Barn being on fire. Known as the "phantom fire," there have been reports from people passing by Stagville late at night who have seen what appears to be the slave quarters blazing on fire. By the time firefighters arrive, there is nothing but darkness around the property, and the buildings show no evidence of fire or heat. Caretakers of the property also report seeing doors open and close on their own, motion detectors being tripped, hearing what sounds like people walking around when the place is empty, and overhearing voices of whispered conversations. Most everyone you meet who has worked or spent time at Stagville agrees that it's haunted.

There is a presence in Stagville that is creepy and forbidding. You are immediately aware that you are not alone. The energy is angry and feels scary even in daylight.

Walking around the property, you may feel your hair stand on end because the energy in the area is so strong. There was some powerful mojo used here on the land, and strong mojo energy lasts for lifetimes. It's a good thing that Stagville is a preserved historic site, because I shudder to think what would happen to any soul who lived on this property now. The energy feels strong and ancient, with a combination of Native American rituals and the traditions of the African slaves who worked the plantation.

Before I enter a place that I know is active with spirits, I conduct a ritual of protection and prepare myself to enter the area. I also bring a small gift, which I offer to the spirits around me, so that they know I come in peace and respect that the place is their home, not mine.

During my visit to Stagville, I sat down outside and made myself comfortable and opened myself up energetically. I asked the spirits of the place to visit with me if they would like to do so. I thought I might get lucky, and the young African American girl might come to visit me. Boy, was I wrong!

Within less than a minute of opening up psychically, spirits surrounded me, and I do mean surrounded. The crowd of people was so large that I couldn't see all of their faces. Instead, I felt the pressure of all of their bodies coming closer to me, wanting to talk. There were so many spirits there that the energy was overwhelming. Spirits try to communicate with us all the time, but most of the time we do not hear them. It takes a lot of energy and an energy source to manifest so that they can be seen, and that is why batteries are so often drained as a spirit must pull energy from the physical plane to allow its spirit body to be seen by the physical eye. This is why when they try to appear, electronics go haywire and other anomalies of this type take place.

In this case, I was alone, sitting outside, and there was nothing electronic for the spirits to pull energy from except me. I became the energy conduit, and once they could sense that I could see and communicate with them, the entire group rushed in. I tried to understand all of their conversations for a few minutes, taking it all in, seeing some of their faces, and feeling their emotions.

I'm an empath (which means that I can feel what others are feeling and I'm very sensitive to surroundings). This can be helpful in my work, but it can also be stressful as I constantly am aware of how other people are feeling about things. In crowded surroundings, such as a mall, it can feel overwhelming with all of the energy swirling around in a cacophony of noise and aggravation. Let's just say you won't find me at the mall doing my Christmas shopping.

The group around me was beginning to feel like a mall experience. They were crowding in closer, talking over each other, and their emotional fears, pain, and anger were taking a toll on me. Knowing that I couldn't take much more before I would begin to shut down the energy flow for protection, it was time to change the situation. I focused my energy and asked the group to hear me. Gaining their attention, I asked for a leader to communicate with me for the group. I looked around expecting one person to step forward, but instead, three women stepped forward.

Two of the women were in spirit form, rather than ghosts. A ghost is the form of a specific person who lived on the earth plane, while many spirits are from other planes of existence beyond the earth plane. Many spirits have never been in human form, and they travel between the planes with greater ease than ghosts are able to do. Many people believe that ghosts stay mainly on the earth plane and can also move to the plane right above the earth plane, but not much further. Spirits, on the other hand, travel through many realms and planes, back and forth with greater ease.

From what I could discern, the spirit women were called into this area during a ritual created by one of the African American enslaved women on the property. She had conducted this ritual to bring some protection to her people during a very difficult time. This woman was the third woman who appeared with the two spirit women. After her death, she remained with them in her ghost form, and the three of them stayed there on the property. I asked her if she still wanted to stay and remain in her ghost form on the land. She replied that she did, that there were still others who remained here in ghost form on the land and that until they found peace and were ready to leave, she would stay and work with the spirit women to heal the people and help them move on. I asked her if there was anything I could do, and she made a request that I return in the spring to visit with her, which I agreed to do.

Stagville! What a place! It's haunted, it's eerie in some places, and it's very active in the paranormal sense. The spirit women that I spoke with reminded me of spirit women that I encountered once in New Orleans, in Congo Square. Many years ago, slaves were allowed to gather in Congo Square on Sunday and play music, dance, sing, and set up a market. That energy can still be felt in Congo Square today, and I felt something similar at Stagville. If you're looking for a hot area of paranormal energy, this is a must-visit on your list of haunted sites in North Carolina.

HAUNTED TOURS IN GREENSBORO, CHARLOTTE, RALEIGH, AND ASHEVILLE

In **Greensboro,** the haunted tour company Carolina History and Haunts offers a 1-mile, 90-minute haunted walking tour described as "Nightmares Around Elm Street." With Dan Riedel as the tour guide, the tour stops at 12 locations. According to Riedel, each of these locations has a haunted history that he's confirmed with the owners and employees of the businesses. Stories include haunted rooms in a hotel, a ghostly woman haunting a theater, and paranormal events at the Guilford County sheriff's office. Reports of ghost sightings on the tour by guests include capturing orbs on film and seeing an apparition appear during a full-moon tour one evening. Carolina History and Haunts also offers haunted tours in **Charlotte** and **Winston-Salem.**

In **Raleigh,** Tobacco Road Tours offers the Raleigh Pub Crawl and Haunted Adventure Tour, which lasts about 2 hours. The tour covers about a mile of haunted downtown Raleigh, covering the state capitol, Mordecai House, Moore Square, and other haunted sites in the city. Ghost stories are shared while walking the streets and visiting various pubs and bars along the way, including Raleigh's first Irish pub.

Asheville is known as the Sedona of the South. Surrounded by some of the oldest mountains in the world, which exude mysterious vortex energy, the city of Asheville and surrounding area hold a deep haunted history. Joshua Warren, radio host, paranormal researcher, and author of *Haunted Asheville,* offers a choice of bus or walking tours around the city. During the haunted tour, Warren shares his paranormal expertise and trains you how to use ghost-hunting equipment, including EMF meters.

CHAPTER 14

RALEIGH

THE FLYING PHOTOGRAPHS OF MARY TURK AT MORDECAI PLANTATION

At around 1792, legislators from North Carolina traveled among several cities to conduct state business and look for a place to designate as the capital city. One of their favorite stops along the way was Isaac Hunter's tavern in Wake County, and rumor has it that one of the main considerations in choosing a site for the capital was to have it located no more than 10 miles from Isaac's tavern so legislators would have a local drinking spot.

Upon hearing this news, competing local tavern owner Joel Lane set out to convince the legislators to buy property near his inn instead. He accomplished this by using a special alcoholic drink he created to sway them in his favor. According to local lore, Lane created a potent libation he named Cherry Bounce, which was made from mashed cherries, sugar, whiskey, and brandy all aged for several weeks. Cherry Bounce became such a popular drink with the visiting legislators that they decided to purchase 1,000 acres from Lane in order to create the capital city. Those forefathers must have loved nature as much as they loved their drink, as they hired designers to plan the city, instructing them to preserve as many trees and create as many parks as possible throughout the city. The rest, as they say, is history.

This leads us to our next haunted adventure: A visit to the Mordecai Plantation. Lane, who later on became a

The Mordecai Plantation was transformed into a Greek revival mansion in 1826.

Wake County Senator, celebrated his successful property transaction with the legislators by building a house for his son Henry on land he owned outside the city limits. Today, that property is one of the oldest neighborhoods in Raleigh.

Henry worked as the clerk of court, and it's been said that he was well-known for his dancing ability. He lived in the house with his wife, Polly, and their four daughters. Sadly, Henry passed away at the young age of 33, and Polly was left to manage the farm. She reportedly did quite well running it all. When she died in 1813, her four daughters were unmarried, and they went to live with their grandfather. When the oldest daughter Margaret married Moses Mordecai, the couple returned to live in the house, and it became known as Mordecai House. The three other sisters came back to the home to live with Margaret and her husband. Moses was an attorney in Raleigh and later became a judge.

Sadly, Margaret passed away and Moses then married her sister, Anne, who raised Margaret's children and had one of her own with Moses. When Moses passed away in 1824, his will requested that the home be renovated and expanded, and in accordance with this request, the home was upgraded in a Greek Revival style. The home sat on a plantation that grew a variety of food crops, as well as a vast selection of herbs and medicinal plants.

In 1907, the General Assembly voted to extend the city's borders, and the Mordecai home and plantation grounds were brought into the city limits. Two buildings were also relocated on Mordecai, which included a chapel and the tavern where future President Andrew Jackson's mother worked. Jackson, the 17th president of the United States, was born in the kitchen of the tavern in 1808.

The land around the home is now known as Mordecai Park and is close to historic Oakwood Cemetery. The home is referred to as Mordecai House, Mordecai Plantation Manor, or Mordecai Mansion. It is listed on the National Register of Historic Places.

The Mordecai House has a long history of being haunted, as do most plantations in North Carolina. The legend states that Mary Willis Mordecai Turk, a descendant of Moses Mordecai, was one of the five generations of Mordecais that lived in the home during the 19th century. It appears that Mary likes to interact with visitors to the home. She appears to many people in the home and has been identified by name. She likes to play the piano and can be seen at times sitting at the piano in the form of a gray mist, which sometimes morphs into the form of a woman wearing period-style dress.

While Mary appears to stay in the house entertaining guests, other ghosts linger around the house and property. Apparitions of Civil War soldiers and nurses have been seen on the property, often reported by local residents, staff, and visitors.

Reports include the ghost of Mary Turk looking out the window, the sounds of a piano playing, and soldiers from the Civil War walking the grounds.

One thing you learn when doing paranormal research is that traumatic events, such as death, war, and severe emotional and physical traumas, like enslaving people, create energies that last for a long time. Some of the ghosts are like time-loop recordings of the event; they make an impression that plays over and over. It's likely that the overwhelming amount of pain endured is part of this recording, as the emotional intensity, fear, and pain experienced by all would make for a strong energy imprint.

There is quite a bit of ghostly activity within the home beyond the very active Mary. After the Civil War, the Mordecai family fortune was essentially gone, and they struggled to recover from their losses. The family at that time consisted of Martha Lane Mordecai and her three daughters. Martha had to sell off much of the land and farm equipment, and the family struggled to survive. The business of simply paying the taxes on the home was often difficult for the family.

One of Martha's daughters married William Turk in 1881. Turk was a Southern Railway executive who had the financial means to pay the taxes on and support the costs of running such a large home. It is thought that without his assistance, it is likely that the family would have lost their home.

The Mordecai family was emotionally attached to their home. When the last generation of the family passed away in 1964, the home was turned into a historic landmark to showcase the beautiful architecture and decor. Mary seems pleased with the company and the attention that she's received over the years. She's even been seen dancing in the moonlight, and she continues to entertain visitors, but other family members in spirit aren't so pleased or welcoming.

One report states that tour guides and tourists were in the home one day when the guide mentioned the individuals by name who had lived in the home. As the guide spoke their names aloud, the pictures of the family members hanging on the walls appeared to float off the walls and sail through the air before falling to the floor. It's not clear what ghost caused the pictures to fly. It could have been a disgruntled family member who was not in the mood to share his home, or perhaps a former slave who did not care for the family and did not wish to hear the stories told by the tour guide. It also has been reported that if someone says something about Mary that is not nice, her photo will slam down. Either Mary has a quick temper or another ghost in the house is very protective of her.

There's also a report that a child who was touring the home saw a man with a scar appear in front of him, only to see him quickly disappear near the Andrew Johnson house. Other visitors have reported seeing candlelight coming from the Johnson house, which disappears a few minutes later. Sounds of hoof beats and the rattling of carriages are also reported in the area. These appear to be time-loop recordings coming from the days when horse-drawn carriages traveled across planks laid down in the mud to help cross the rough and muddy roads of Raleigh.

Because of the interaction between the Mordecai ghosts and visitors, this house goes on my list as being one that would be great for a séance. Communication would likely be achieved with the spirits in the house.

The State Capitol building in Raleigh is considered one of the most haunted capitols in the United States.

CHAPTER 15

RALEIGH

GOVERNOR STILL WORKING AT THE STATE CAPITOL BUILDING

Paranormal activity in the North Carolina state capitol has been reported since the late 1800s, and the city boasts that it has the most haunted capitol in the country. There are numerous reports by security officers investigating strange sounds of glass breaking and people walking and talking in the building after hours, only to find the rooms empty. The experiences don't stop with security—several former governors and their staff members have reported their encounters with spirits while working late nights in the building.

Several years back, I spent the night in the state capitol with my investigative team, The Rowan Society, along with several other paranormal researchers and ghost hunters. The investigation was organized and led by Anne Poole, who has a paranormal research group of her own here in North Carolina. Anne is also involved in the research of the Lost Colony of Roanoke.

Is the capitol haunted? I can answer with a resounding yes! After receiving special permission for an evening of research, all the alarms in the building were disconnected due to the large number of people involved in the ghost hunt. As we entered the library and looked around, I noticed the ghostly form of a man in the corner. As he moved closer toward me, the security alarms went off, although this was deemed impossible since they were disconnected.

During the debriefing afterward with security and other investigative team members, it was determined that we had seen the ghost of Zebulon Vance, a former governor of North Carolina who is reputed to still haunt the building. Employees and visitors to the capitol continue to report new and recurring incidences with ghosts to this day, adding to this Raleigh landmark's haunted reputation.

Before meeting the ghost of Governor Vance in the library, we had also spent time downstairs in a room where we all smelled tobacco smoke. The capitol has a no-smoking policy, but the smell was as strong as if someone were standing next to us smoking. Several members of our research team spent time in the geologist's office during the investigation, where they reported hearing voices in the room.

Zebulon Vance was a state legislator at 24, a congressman at 28, and a Confederate colonel at 31, with his own company called the Rough and Ready Guards. Vance was elected governor at the age of 32. He served three terms as the governor of North Carolina and was a United States senator for 15 years. He was originally an attorney and practiced law in Asheville before being elected solicitor for Buncombe County.

During the Civil War, Vance had been on the side of keeping slavery in place. In 1865, he was placed in prison. Upon his release, he practiced law in Charlotte and ran for state senate. He won the election but was unable to take the seat in 1870 due to the 14th amendment, which states in Section 3: "No person shall be a Senator or Representative in Congress, or elector of President and Vice President, or hold any office, civil or military, under the United States, or under any State, who, having previously taken an oath, as a member of Congress, or as an officer of the United States, or as a member of any State legislature, or as an executive or judicial officer of any State, to support the Constitution of the United States, shall have engaged in insurrection or rebellion against the same, or given aid or comfort to the enemies thereof. But Congress may, by a vote of two-thirds of each House, remove such disability."

He fought against this amendment and won, and was seated in 1872. He then ran for governor in 1876 and brought new energy to the state, resuming railroad construction, promoting industry, escorting the last of the federal troops out of the state, and creating a more stable financial structure for the state. He spoke about moving forward to create a "New South" and looking forward to new progress, rather than focusing on what had occurred in the past. Vance died in office on April 14, 1894, and was buried in Asheville.

I've gone back to visit the capitol several other times, but it's completely different during the daytime, as the amount of people in the building makes it virtually impossible to hear anything out-of-the-ordinary. The night of the investigation we were able to cover every square inch of the building, and we had the entire night to do so. During the day, the tours are conducted only through certain sections of the building. One fun anomaly, though, is to stand in the rotunda area. Due to the design of the room, there is one area where you can stand and quietly whisper something that will be heard loud and clear around the room; it's fascinating. I've often wondered how many freshmen legislators are taken to that spot and asked a question that they might not have shared publicly with others, only to discover the anomaly for themselves upon answering.

You don't even have to enter the capitol building to meet the ghosts. Orbs are reported frequently on the grounds of the capitol, by the windows, and around many of the statues on the lawn. The best time to walk around the area to see orbs and ghosts is in the late evening, when things are quiet and you can stroll around the lawn in the peaceful night. Bring a recorder along, as you might be surprised to find the number of EVPs that you'll pick up.

ESP AND PARAPSYCHOLOGY AT THE RHINE RESEARCH CENTER

The Society of Psychical Research (SPR) was founded in London in 1882 to study paranormal phenomena including telepathy, hauntings, and the effects of spiritualism. SPR became the model for other paranormal research organizations to adopt, and in 1885, the American Society for Psychical Research (ASPR) began its work. In 1911, Stanford University became the first American institution to study ESP (extrasensory perception) and PK (psychokinesis). In 1927, Joseph (J. B.) and Louisa Rhine joined Duke University, and in 1930, J. B. began to undertake the study of ESP, which was referred to at the time as psychical research, making Duke the second institution in the country to engage in critical study of psychic phenomena. ESP is the psi ability to detect energy or receive information through means other than the five senses or direct communication. Working with William McDougall, J. B. began his work by studying mediums in order to search for evidence of the afterlife.

J. B. Rhine used zener cards (a set of five cards with a different symbol on each: circle, star, wavy lines, square, and a Greek cross) to test students at Duke for their ESP abilities. The cards were shuffled, and students were asked to guess which symbol was on the card drawn. If they tested above the average norm of lucky guesses, they were considered to be accessing some form of clairvoyance. Rhine also used dice machines to see if some students could move the objects through their thoughts in order to gather statistical data. By 1935, the Duke Parapsychology Lab was formed, where experiments grew and the science of parapsychology was created. Parapsychology is the study of phenomena including telepathy, PK, TK (telekinesis), clairvoyance, and other psi abilities.

Rhine was instrumental in bringing this information to public attention through the publication of his books, including *Extra Sensory Perception, New Frontiers of the Mind,* and *Parapsychology: Frontier Science of the Mind,* as well as publishing the *Journal of Parapsychology.* Rhine eventually broke ties with Duke and established the Foundation for the Research on the Nature of Man (FRNM). In 1995, the institute was renamed in honor of J. B. and is now known as the Rhine Research Center.

The Rhine Research Center focuses on consciousness research, and studies including remote viewing, PK, TK, and telepathy are conducted. The Rhine ESP/Parapsychology Museum showcases the equipment that was used in parapsychological studies and research over the past 70 years. The museum is available for tours by appointment and is located in Durham, North Carolina.

The Carolina Inn oozes southern charm, so it's no surprise that some guests never want to leave.

CHAPTER 16

CHAPEL HILL

SO COMFORTABLE THAT GUESTS AND GHOSTS NEVER WANT TO LEAVE THE CAROLINA INN

The prominent Carolina Inn was built in 1924 to attend to visitors and alumni of the University of North Carolina. The architecture of the building was patterned after that of George Washington's home in Mount Vernon.

The ballroom of the Carolina Inn is considered to be one of the most haunted areas of the inn. Perhaps it's second only to Suite 252, where Dr. William Jacocks lived for almost 20 years. He's been reported to be a friendly ghost and very welcoming. Guests report that even in the absence of fresh flowers in the room they will be welcomed with an overwhelming floral scent. Others will be greeted with a strong cologne smell.

Dr. Jacocks is known to be a fun-loving prankster. He reportedly enjoys playing tricks at the inn, including locking guests out of Room 252. The local lore states that at one time, the door had to be taken off its hinges because it was so stuck it wouldn't open under any circumstances. Electronic locks were installed in the hotel in 1990, but there continue to be repeated complaints of the door refusing to unlock.

Other guests have reported all sorts of paranormal activity in the room, including curtains being pulled open in a wild manner and icy spots in the room, even though the air-conditioning is not running. Staff at the inn report seeing a man appear in a black suit with a blue overcoat and knit hat walking around the inn. He reportedly goes from door to door touching and jiggling the knobs. Some guests have reported hearing the sound and opening the door to see what the man wants, only to watch him disappear before their eyes.

Some reports claim that there are up to 20 ghosts at the inn. Witnesses have heard the sound of a piano playing in areas where there is no music or musical instruments. Others have heard footsteps in empty rooms. Voices have been heard, orbs recorded, and sightings of ghosts are reported around the inn on a frequent basis.

The inn's owners are comfortable with the reports and host a yearly Halloween event that includes a ghost tour and an overnight stay and dinner to discuss the activity in the hotel. The ghosts have all been reported to be friendly and enjoy the inn so much that they refuse to leave.

The Carolina Inn is owned by the University of North Carolina and listed on the National Register of Historic Places, so once again, you know it's going onto my National Register of Haunted Places list. The inn is full of yummy Southern hospitality, and the staff is warm and welcoming; it's no surprise to me that guests would want to stay for a lifetime and beyond. With 184 cheery and beautifully decorated rooms and a wonderful location by the university, it's often referred to as the University's Living Room.

During my visit to the inn, I enjoyed walking around the property. The most widely reported incidents of ghostly activities are inside the building, but to my surprise, where I felt the most activity was around one of the doors.

As I walked through this door, I was looking down at the ground. I had felt a strange energy in this area, and while focusing on this energy I nearly dropped my camera and reached out quickly to grab the strap. While doing so, it felt as if I bumped solidly into a person. Startled, I stepped back and looked up to apologize to the person whom I had run into, only to find myself completely alone. I looked all throughout the room, but there was no one to be found. The entity that I bumped into had felt as solid as a man. Unfortunately, whoever it was, it had no desire to communicate further with me and did not appear again. Perhaps I had startled it as much as it had startled me. One never knows quite what will happen next when ghost hunting, and the majority of the time, it seems to happen when you least expect it.

THE BROWN LADY OF CHOWAN UNIVERSITY

Chowan University, in Murfreesboro, North Carolina, was founded in 1848 as the Chowan Baptist Female Institute, a four-year women's college. Legend states that during the Civil War, a female student at Chowan was engaged to her beloved, who left to fight in the war. Reportedly he died in battle, and she later died of a broken heart.

Since her death, her ghost has been seen walking through buildings and appearing in the halls around the university. She most often appears in a mist and is seen wearing a brown dress, which has earned her the nickname "The Brown Lady." Reports of her appearance began shortly after her death, and the staff noticed other strange occurrences, such as piles of leaves gathered in the hallways after the building had been locked and secured in the evening.

The legend of the Brown Lady continued to grow, as did her appearances, which led to a yearly event at the college dubbed "The Brown Lady Festival" in the 1940s and 1950s. During the festival, a student would be nominated to dress up as the Brown Lady. The celebration culminated with partygoers walking from the college campus to the nearby Wise Family Cemetery. No one knows the name of the Brown Lady or if she is buried in this nearby cemetery. Perhaps the students journeyed to the Wise Family Cemetery hoping to help the Brown Lady find a final resting place.

Chowan University is a Christian school with approximately 1,000 students in attendance from more than 20 states and foreign countries. The Brown Lady continues to make an appearance at Chowan University, and the school acknowledges this fact. She is a well-known and recognized part of the university and its history. Chowan now states that she returned from the dead to "test the loyalty of the students." Others feel that she visits to instill a sense of pride and eternal love.

CHAPTER 17

FOUR OAKS

THE HAUNTING BENTONVILLE BATTLEFIELD DRIVING TOUR

The Bentonville Battlefield was the scene of the most major battle held in North Carolina during the Civil War.

Bentonville. As soon as I knew I was writing *Ghost Hunting North Carolina,* I knew this story would have to be in the book. Bentonville is a battlefield. It's hard to find a North Carolina native who has not heard of this battle. But I'm getting ahead of myself here; let's start at the beginning, back before the Civil War took its toll on the area.

In 1855, John and Amy Harper built a home, which is referred to as the Harper House. Located in the village of Bentonville, the area was surrounded by open fields and lush pine forests. Bentonville was a marketplace for naval stores, selling mostly tar, pitch, and turpentine. The Harpers had moved from West Virginia to North Carolina, where John owned almost 800 acres of land. Harper had cleared almost 100 acres of the land, which he used for farmland. The other forested acres were used to harvest tar, pitch, and turpentine from the pine trees. During this period of hard work and perseverance, John, Amy, and their nine children most likely would never have guessed that only 10 years later, their home, along with several others, would be front and center of a battlefield. The Harpers were touched by the war before the battle started, as their 16-year-old son, Martin, had joined the Confederate army and was wounded in battle in 1862. He had returned home to recover and heal and left again in 1864 to rejoin his unit.

During Sherman's march on North Carolina in 1865, Union troops took over the Harper House and turned it into a hospital for the troops. The Harpers and seven of their children were given the choice of staying in the upstairs section of the home to care for wounded Union soldiers or to leave immediately with nowhere to stay. They chose to stay in the home and care for wounded soldiers.

The Battle of Bentonville was one of the last major engagements of the Civil War. The battle was waged over 6,000 acres, and the number of soldiers made this the largest battle fought in North Carolina. Around 80,000 men fought in this battle, with 60,000 being from the Union and 21,000 men from the Confederacy. The entire battle lasted from March 19th through the 21st, but the devastation left behind has lasted for lifetimes.

The casualties of this battle hovered around 4,200 men killed, wounded, or presumed missing. During this three-day battle, more than 500 soldiers were cared for in the Harper House.

On March 22, the Union army defeated the Confederate army. The Union troops left the area, taking their wounded with them. The entire village of Bentonville was devastated, and the locals who had remained in the area through the battle had little food or medical resources to care for the wounded Confederate soldiers. They also struggled to bury the remains of more than 360 Confederate soldiers and 140 Union soldiers.

Many of the fallen men died on the battlefield and were buried where they fell. Local residents buried the rest of the dead after the Union soldiers and the battle moved on. Twenty Confederate soldiers were buried in a mass grave next to the Harper family cemetery.

When you visit the Harper House today, it is set up to look as it did during the Civil War; the first floor displays what a field hospital looked like during the war, while the second-floor exhibits traditional furnishings where the family lived.

Union soldiers buried in the area were moved in 1867 to national cemeteries established by the U.S. government, and those in Bentonville were moved to the Raleigh National Cemetery. Confederate fallen were ignored by the government and left in poorly marked graves for another 30 years before an attempt was made to note the graves with some dignity.

The best way to visit the battlefield is to take the 10-mile driving tour, which has historic markers and exhibits that explain what happened in each area along this drive in regards to the battle. Each marker contains significant coverage of the battle. As you move from one marker to the next, you truly get a good feel for what this battle entailed and how much everyone involved suffered. At one marker I was overcome with grief and strong emotion. It was the Confederate North Carolina Junior Reserves memorial. The Confederate army was on its last legs and in desperate need of anyone who could serve, so they expanded the age range for new recruits. The Reserve included boys as young as 17. These young men were unprepared for this fierce battle but did their best. Some reports state that boys even younger had joined to fight. General Hardee of the Confederate army was involved in Bentonville, leading a counterattack to protect the Mill Creek Bridge. General Hardee had a 16-year-old son named Willie. Against the general's wishes, Willie joined the battle on March 21 and was mortally wounded, dying three days later.

Soldiers from the Civil War are still seen here on the battlefield. Reenactments of the battle are held here on the field, which seems to trigger the ghostly appearances even more.

A quote on this marker reads: "It was in a good wood for skirmishing, with little or no undergrowth. We had a regular Indian fight of it behind the trees. They charged my line twice, but were both times driven back. That night, the whole skirmish line kept up an almost continuous firing as they expected our Army to leave. That, together with the scamps trying to creep up on us in the dark, kept us up all night." This quote is from Major Walter Clark of the North Carolina Junior Reserves, describing the action on March 20, 1865.

What's left of the Village of Bentonville is the Harper House and the markers of the battlefield. I had a hard time finding anyone who wanted to talk about the haunted activity in the area, though it is often reported. Some people agreed to speak with me about what they had personally experienced or heard reported about haunted activity in the area, but they also asked to remain anonymous. The reports are horrific; many report that if you are in certain areas of the battlefield on moonlit nights, you can smell the decaying bodies that were left on the field and hear moans and groans from the wounded soldiers who lay dying. People report hearing men running, shouting, and at times screaming in battle, with the roar of cannons and rifles going off at the same time. Many people have seen the ghosts of the men as they shoot and get shot and fall down dying. Many of the descriptions of the ghostly battle scenes reported remind me of Gettysburg.

Several people discussed the hauntings at the Harper House with me, though officially the staff does not discuss any haunted activity. Witnesses claim, though, that there is a large amount of ghostly activity at the Harper House, including lights floating around the house at night, cold spots inside the house and around the property, and Union soldiers walking around at all hours of the night and day. The people who were willing to tell me their stories are adamant that there is ghostly activity in the area. They also report seeing bonfires in the vicinity around the Harper House and the surrounding battlefield that appear and disappear as quickly as they form. I was also told a story in confidence that there is an apparition of a soldier often seen in the window of the Harper House who is holding a bucket with one hand while the stump of his other arm drips blood into the bucket.

The nearest town is Four Oaks, which has a population of around 2,000 people. The cemetery may be the best area to look for paranormal activity. There were several areas in which I felt overwhelming grief and sadness. I heard voices several times in the distance of men speaking, and smelled smoke in a couple of places, as well. Of all of the places in North Carolina, if you feel that you have some psychic ability and are wondering if you can sense ghosts, this would be the best testing ground to try out your abilities, as almost anywhere you walk, the chance of encountering some paranormal activity is pretty high.

I'd also recommend scheduling a visit to observe the reenactment of the Battle of Bentonville. Reenactments are known to stir up the emotional energy in the area, and ghosts often appear during these types of events. Reenactments are held every March, and 2025 commemorated the 160th anniversary of the battle.

The Page-Walker Hotel in Cary, North Carolina, as it stands today *(Photo by Kala Ambrose)*

CHAPTER 18

CARY

PROHIBITION AND THE GHOST OF THE PAGE-WALKER HOTEL

Cary, North Carolina, is a suburban town located in the middle of the Triangle area between Raleigh, Durham, and Chapel Hill. The town is consistently voted one of the safest cities in America. Known as a family-oriented community with excellent schools, Cary is filled with manicured lawns, planned subdivisions including a community designed by Martha Stewart, and soccer moms galore. Cary is friendly, pleasant, and dedicated to preserving the natural surroundings with a variety of public parks, walking trails, and greenways to enjoy. With a population of around 130,000, Cary rolls up the sidewalks at night and is one of the most peaceful and quiet towns in the area.

As the old saying goes, "Still waters run deep." It's the quiet ones that most often have the most intriguing stories to tell, for Cary has more ghosts than many residents realize, including several that lead an active life when the sun goes down.

Cary originally consisted of 1 square mile and was established around 1850, during the construction of the railroad in North Carolina. Before the railroad came through, the area was called Bradford's Ordinary. Bradford's Ordinary was actually just an inn run by John Bradford, but since little else but farmland existed in the territory, most people referred to the entire area as Bradford's Ordinary. The arrival of the railroad brought commerce and industry and attracted people to settle in the area.

In 1854, Allison Francis Page, a businessman who went by the name Frank, moved to this area and purchased 300 acres by the railroad. In 1868, Frank Page established this area as the town of Cary. This area today is known as downtown Cary. Page created some of the roads, established a post office, and built a general store and a hotel.

Page, who also became Cary's first mayor, incorporated the town in 1871, naming it Cary in honor of Samuel Fenton Cary, a temperance leader. Samuel Cary had come to Raleigh to speak about the values of temperance. Page shared those beliefs and so named the town in honor of Cary and his temperance campaign.

Page was reportedly fundamentally religious and dogmatic in his beliefs. It was said that he disapproved of "theater going, cursing, dancing, card playing, and most of all, drinking." He so believed in temperance that he established the town of Cary as a "dry" community. As Cary grew, many religious people settled there, and it's likely that they did not feel comfortable speaking about ghosts or other paranormal occurrences, even if they experienced them personally. Believe it or not, Cary remained a dry community for almost 100 years, until 1964. Even then the town did not willingly embrace the sale of alcohol. There are reports that say that Cary had to be prodded by the State Attorney General, who had to issue a formal statement to the town leaders to remind them that the town's dry charter was invalid since Wake County had voted for the sale of alcohol back in 1937.

As Frank Page and his wife, Catherine Raboteau Page, settled into the area, they built their home behind the hotel they had constructed near the railroad. The Civil War decimated their family wealth, as it did so many others, and there are some reports that Mrs. Page was seen creating drapes made from worthless $100 Confederate bills. In this home, Frank worked hard and rebuilt his wealth while Catherine raised their eight children, three girls and five boys. Their son Walter Hines Page established a newspaper, which later evolved into the *Raleigh News and Observer.* Walter Page eventually partnered with Frank Doubleday to establish the publishing company Doubleday, Page & Co. Page later became the Ambassador to Great Britain and participated in establishing North Carolina State University.

The Page home burned down in 1970, and the Town Hall now stands on the land where the house once stood. Statues of young children at play have been placed near the Town Hall where the home was located. Several local people who walk through downtown in the evening have reported seeing orbs floating around these statues after office hours when the town is quiet. The orbs reportedly fly around the statues and then move on, circling around the buildings in this area.

In the national panic of 1873, which is also referred to as the Depression of 1873, most of the businesses in Cary closed. Frank Page moved his businesses during this time and sold his hotel to J.R. Walker. While there are many legacies of Page's work in the town, the one that stands out most is the Page-Walker Hotel. The French Empire architectural style of the hotel is quite impressive, especially when considering that during the time it was built the town consisted of about 300 people. Beautifully restored, the Page-Walker Hotel is now an arts center hosting concerts, classes, and weddings. Many believe that it's also haunted.

Years ago, I encountered a ghost during my visit to the Page-Walker Hotel. This led me to research the history of the hotel to determine what type of activities had gone on in the hotel since its inception. The building had been in operation as a hotel, a boarding house, and in its last incarnation, as a private residence. In 1980, the building was put up for sale and remained on the market for years.

At this point, the building began to deteriorate rapidly, with rain causing the majority of the damage to the interior. If it had not been for a concerned and tenacious group of citizens known as The Friends of the Page-Walker Hotel, who decided to save the hotel as a piece of history, there would be no ghost story to tell, for it's highly likely that at the rate the hotel was declining, it would have been torn down.

I still remember the first time I visited the hotel. It was to inquire about a course being offered at the center. I entered the building and walked up to the reception area, where an elderly lady was working at the desk. As I approached to inquire about registration for the class, I saw that she was on the phone, and she held up a finger to me in the universal sign that signaled me to be quiet and wait. I smiled to her and stood quietly to the side so that she could continue her conversation.

A few minutes later, I was still waiting and she was still talking, and I grew bored and restless. I began to walk around the center to see what it looked like. I entered what is called the Main Gallery Room, and by the looks of the room, I presumed that this was where the course I was interested in would be held. I walked around, taking my time looking things over.

So many times in ghost hunting, ghosts appear when you least expect them. As I was standing there in the room, a mist began to appear before me, gradually turning into the apparition of a man. He turned around, looking past me. He made a motion as if he was trying to close a door, but there was no door where we stood. What was most interesting about his appearance was that I could smell alcohol around him when he manifested, and it appeared to me that he had passed away while drunk. He seemed to be unaware that he was dead and he was stuck in a limbo where he still appeared to be under the influence of alcohol.

At first I thought that he was a time-loop apparition, but my opinion changed as he looked at me and gave me a mischievous grin. Many people are scared when they see a ghost, but since I've had a lifetime of experience, it's not that unsettling when they appear. He appeared to be a nice man, just stuck in the drunken state in which he died. As I was about to attempt to communicate with him, the lady who had been on the phone called out to me to say that she was off the phone. I turned my head to reply to her that I was on my way, and when I turned back to look at the ghost, he was gone. The center was preparing to close for the day, so I was unable to continue any further attempts at communication.

The drunken state of this ghost was of course most interesting to me since history shows that Cary was a dry town for most of its existence. The town has only had 40-plus years of legal alcohol. The appearance of this man was from a time long before 1960, so one has to wonder how he obtained the alcohol and what led to his demise.

During the late 1800s through the 1960s, religion and Prohibition continued to be a unifying theme of the town, and the churches were said to be strict in their beliefs. Local legends state that the Cary Baptist Church in 1914 expelled 24 members because they had been dancing and had not been attending services. If anyone was enjoying a drink of alcohol or seeing ghosts, they definitely weren't comfortable sharing this information with others for fear of retribution.

Cary began its renaissance in the 1980s. No longer a dry town, the establishment of the Research Triangle Park (RTP) next to Cary created one of the most prominent high-tech research and development centers in the country. Compared often to Silicon Valley, RTP was created with the cooperation of state and local governments and major universities. This led to a population explosion as housing expanded in the area in a town once crowded with churches on almost every corner.

Evidence of Page's influence can be seen all around Cary, including the first public school in North Carolina, which he established. The school was originally called Cary Academy and operated as a private boarding school. It has now been converted into the Cary Community Arts Center. Local lore states that when it was still operating as a school, custodians and several students reported seeing and hearing the ghosts of a girl and a boy in various parts of the building. Several students also reported the feeling of being watched when they were walking down an empty hallway alone.

Cary also has a cemetery known as Hillcrest, which is the final resting place of many of the old Cary families, with familiar local names such as Page, Harrison, and Jones listed on the headstones. Hillcrest is a small cemetery owned by the town, and private residences border the cemetery on all sides. Local legends state that there is the ghost of a man, which many describe as "the farmer," that appears on occasion in the cemetery. Dressed in period clothing from the early 19th century, the farmer appears by the largest tree in the cemetery, often standing there with his hand resting on the tree. He seems to be a caretaker of the cemetery and has been known to appear during funerals to pay his respects. When he appears, he's quiet, stands silently by the tree, and just observes what is going on around him.

As I began to open up to people in Cary and share my experience at the Page-Walker Hotel, I was surprised at how many had ghost stories of their own in the area, including several having felt a presence at Page-Walker and near the Town Hall. It appeared that my willingness to speak first and share my experiences allowed others to feel comfortable in sharing their personal paranormal experiences, local legends, and folklore.

Some of the old-timers whose families have lived in Cary for decades still don't feel comfortable talking about their stories publicly due to their religious beliefs. They feel it's disrespectful to discuss paranormal experiences.

Over the years, Cary has evolved into a vibrant, active community that celebrates a variety of cultures. From Turkish festivals to the Hindu celebration of Diwali, the Spring Daze and Lazy Daze Festival, and Herbfest at the Page-Walker Center, the town has expanded and opened up to a variety of new experiences.

At Hillcrest Cemetery in Cary, the ghost of a farmer is seen by the largest tree on the grounds.

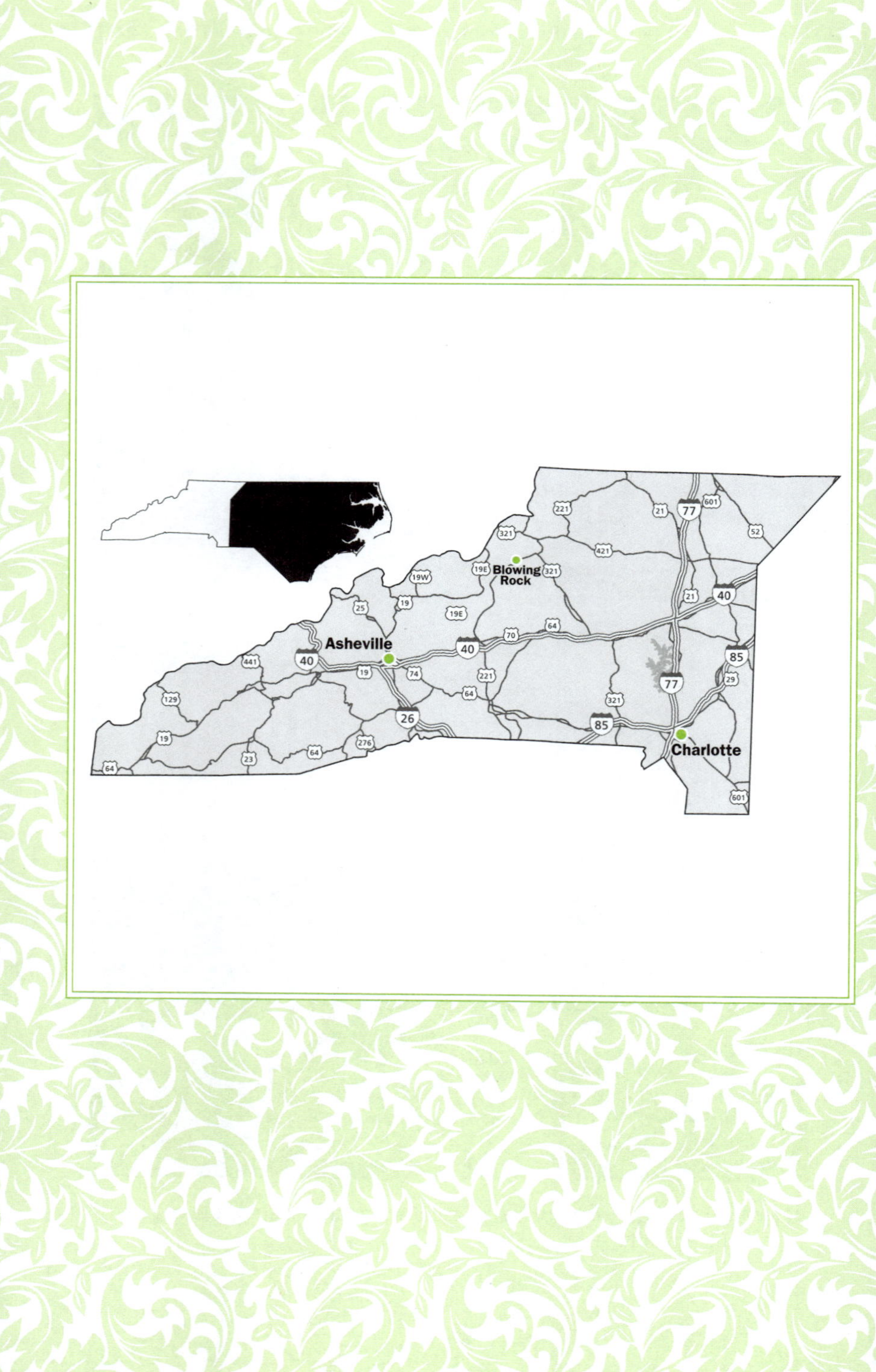

Blowing Rock
Asheville
Charlotte
221
21
77
601
52
321
421
19E
19W
19
25
40
64
70
441
74
85
29
129
26
276
23

WEST CAROLINA

The Blue Ridge Mountains and the Foothills

View of Biltmore Estate with backdrop of the Blue Ridge Mountains

CHAPTER 19

ASHEVILLE

THE VANDERBILTS WHO NEVER LEFT BILTMORE ESTATE

If you've spent any time in western North Carolina, you'll understand why I keep referring to the irrefutable beauty of the mountains. One of my favorite views in Asheville is from the Sunset Terrace of the Grove Park Inn, where the city lights twinkle at night.

My second favorite view is the mountain backdrop against the Biltmore estate. Where does one begin to describe such a grand site, both architecturally and naturally? This view may be the most perfect in the area, looking out at wave after wave of Blue Ridge Mountains in their grandeur.

George Vanderbilt, grandson of Cornelius Vanderbilt, must have agreed, for after touring the location, he bought 125,000 acres and built Biltmore estate. The estate is the largest home in the United States, with more than four acres of floor space and over 250 rooms, including 34 bedrooms, 43 bathrooms, and 65 fireplaces.

Vanderbilt wanted to create a symphony of balance between the natural backdrop of the mountains, the acres surrounding his estate, and the architectural design of his home. He hired Richard Morris Hunt to design the home in a French Renaissance Chateau style, and the effect is superb, as the home is prominent and striking and blends beautifully with the mountains behind it. The steeply pitched roof of the home creates a wonderful style mirroring the mountain range.

It's difficult to imagine how many people it took to create this estate. In order to have the supplies needed at hand, the estate created its own brick factory, woodworking shop, and even established a 3-mile rail system to move materials to the building site. Over the years, more than 11 million bricks were made to build the home.

Vanderbilt had a strong artistic taste, and he traveled with Hunt through Europe and Asia, collecting the artwork of Renoir, Lorrain, Pellegrini, Boldini, Sargent, and Whistler, along with furniture designed by Chippendale. There are Chinese goldfish bowls from the Ming Dynasty, several 16th-century tapestries and Persian rugs, and a chess set that once belonged to Napoleon. The opulence is apparent in every room of the home, with my favorite room being the library.

In addition to showcasing exquisite taste, the home was the most technologically advanced of its time. The house was centrally heated and had electricity, using some of Thomas Edison's first light bulbs. Biltmore had indoor plumbing, a telephone, a fire alarm system, and an intercom system to speak with the servants. There's also a gym, bowling alley, and indoor swimming pool. No detail was overlooked in the design of this home.

Eight thousand acres are still owned by the estate today and include striking formal and informal gardens, which were designed by Frederick Law Olmsted. Olmsted is known as the "American father of landscape architecture." He's most famous for designing Central Park in New York, as well as designing landscapes for Yale, Stanford, and Boston University. Vanderbilt wanted Olmsted to give the estate a European country feel, while also revering the natural beauty of North Carolina. Olmsted succeeded on all accounts. The formal gardens include a 4-acre English walled garden, a 16th-century Italian garden with three reflecting pools, and a tree-lined road along the 3-mile entrance to the home.

Olmsted created a beautiful nursery to care for a wide variety of flora, and I enjoyed touring the nursery as much as the home. If you enjoy gardening, you'll find it to be a greenhouse of dreams, as the variety of species included, along with the space to care for them, is incredible. Tulips, roses, and plants of all types can be found here, and in the winter months, more than 1,000 poinsettias are grown and then used to decorate inside the estate. Olmstead worked indigenous plants into his designs, including azaleas, mountain laurel, and rhododendron.

Vanderbilt was 25 years old when he purchased the property in the late 1880s. In 1895, he officially opened the estate with an elaborate housewarming party for family and friends on Christmas Eve. The house was his dream for a country retreat where he could pursue his "passion for art, literature, and horticulture." In 1898, he married Edith Dresser, and after their honeymoon they moved to the estate. Even after they moved in, work continued on the home.

Edith and George were very much in love, and it was said that they complemented each other very well. They had one daughter, Cornelia, who was born in the home, and it appears that they had an idyllic life enjoying the best the world had to offer.

In 1914, George had an appendectomy and died from complications resulting from the surgery. Shortly after his death, servants in the home noticed that Edith began spending a lot of time in the library and that while she was there, she was speaking out loud to George's spirit. At first, they dismissed this act as a woman in grief over the death of her beloved husband. They assumed that after a period of time, she would move on from her grief, after finishing her discussions of things that she had wished to say to George that she had been unable to before his untimely death.

Instead, the opposite happened. Edith continued her daily conversations with George, and during this time servants in the home began to notice the presence of his spirit, mostly in the library and in his favorite sitting room on the second floor. According to the legends, many of the servants heard footsteps and then saw an apparition of George around the home.

After Edith died, the legends continued, as the servants reported hearing the voices of both Edith and George now conversing in the library. Perhaps now that they were joined again in the afterlife, they were able to pick up where they left off and enjoy their time together in their treasured home. Reports continue today from staff and visitors who hear voices in the library and a few other rooms.

There are quite a few ghost stories about Biltmore, which some locals shared with me during my visit to Asheville. Several employees answered my questions as well, as long as I agreed to keep their identity off the record. Officially, Biltmore does not discuss haunted or paranormal activity in the home or on the property. Also, photography is not allowed inside the home. The only spirits that they will officially discuss are the spirits of the wine made at the Biltmore winery.

Tales of ghostly sightings and experiences continue to be reported by employees and visitors to the home, and it appears that the ghosts of George and Edith are not the only spirits in the home. A headless orange cat, for example, has been seen on the property for years, running around only to disappear in full sight of many people at the same time. There is also a report of a maid who appears holding a tray of glasses filled with Champagne who then disappears before the visitors; others have seen a butler holding a tray.

One of the most haunted areas on the Biltmore Estate is the indoor swimming pool, where staff and visitors often hear a voice coming from the drain in the center of the pool. The public tour of the home leads you into the indoor pool room, but the pool is drained. Many people report feeling uneasy in this room, and some claim to have seen a dark, shadow-type figure there. Almost everyone I spoke with about the Biltmore house had a story or experience to share about what they felt or have been told about the pool room, including hearing someone laughing so loud that it bordered on sounding hysterical, and several people have seen the image of a body floating facedown in the pool. There does not appear to be a record of anyone drowning in the pool, though there have been several theories that perhaps one of the servant's children may have drowned. Others state that it is not a body floating in the pool, but rather several dark shadow figures that are moving around the pool and when they are seen, the pool appears full of water. There are also several reports of seeing a lady dressed in black walking around the pool area.

The swimming pool room did feel creepy to me as I visited on a tour. Our tour guide moved us quickly through this room, and I didn't hear or see anything while there and was only in the room for a brief time. I did, however, sense a ghostly presence in the kitchen area while on the tour. The ghost there made its presence known for a minute and then retreated. She was an older woman wearing an apron and had her hair pulled back in a very messy and disheveled bun. She appeared to be watching the people come and go and was very concerned that nothing should be touched in the kitchen. She appeared to be angry and in a bad mood. The kitchen is set up with displays of how it was used when the servants worked there, and most likely the ghost would be one of those servants who worked in the kitchen.

The other two rooms where I felt the most energy were the library and the first room you enter at Biltmore, which has glass-roofed windows flooding light into the circular area of the room, where grand parties were thrown. Both rooms were electric with energy, all of a very positive nature. This is how Biltmore feels overall; beautiful, inspiring, and at times unbelievable in the sheer majesty of the gardens, the mountains, and the home's architecture and design, which are a veritable feast for all of the senses.

JOSHUA P. WARREN'S ASHEVILLE TOURISM CENTER AND FREE MUSEUM

Joshua Warren, radio host, paranormal researcher, and author of more than 12 books, including *How to Hunt Ghosts,* has opened the Joshua P. Warren's Asheville Tourism Center and Free Museum in a building that once housed the county jail. Located in downtown Asheville, the museum is full of macabre exhibits and paranormal artifacts and has already reported a ghostly experience in the museum itself.

In January 2011, shortly after the museum opened, a staff member encountered a full-body apparition of a man inside the museum. After describing the man, the museum historian discovered that on the same date 87 years earlier, a Buncombe County sheriff and former chief of police named John Lyerly died by suicide, shooting himself in the building. Historic records state that Lyerly was not the friendliest of characters, and his presence today still feels dark.

Historic exhibits include a model of the Battery Park Hotel, where Helen Clevenger was murdered in 1936, and an exhibit on the tale of Will Harris, who committed Asheville's largest mass murder spree.

The old jail building has bars on the windows, and the history of crime and punishment in Asheville is shared, including how hangings were handled in the town. Other interesting stories include Asheville's connection to the Hope Diamond and Warren's research on the Brown Mountain Lights. There's also a psychomanteum room, where visitors can sit in a dark room and face a mirror in order to see and communicate with the spiritual realms.

CHAPTER 20

ASHEVILLE

THE GENTLE TOUCH FROM THE PINK LADY AT THE GROVE PARK INN

The Palm Court is located inside the Main Inn area of the Grove Park Inn. *(Photo by Kala Ambrose)*

I first visited the Grove Park Inn in Asheville in 1998. I had not previously heard of the inn until some of our neighbors invited us to tag along with them for a weekend there. We arrived at check-in to find that we all had rooms in a part of the hotel called the Main Inn.

The Grove Park Inn is a stunning hotel built from granite quarried from the surrounding mountains. The granite has a mixture of quartz crystal inside. Quartz crystal can absorb, hold, and amplify energy at a greater level. An example of how energy can be magnified is the vortex that

Gary Spivey opened at the Star Hotel, connecting with the quartz crystal in the land, which energized both the land and the crystals. When quartz is in the stone of a building like the Grove Park, it radiates with the energy of the people who work and visit the inn.

Whenever I visit the Grove Park, I have an "instant experience" that is very positive in nature. Each time I enter the inn, I can feel the vibrational energy coming from the stone structure, and it resonates with the happy energy of the many guests who have visited over the decades.

A partial list of famous people who have stayed at the Grove Park Inn includes F. Scott Fitzgerald, Will Rogers, George Gershwin, Harry Houdini, Thomas Edison, and Henry Ford. Presidents who have stayed at the inn include William Taft, Woodrow Wilson, Calvin Coolidge, Herbert Hoover, Franklin Roosevelt, Dwight Eisenhower, Richard Nixon, George H. W. Bush, Bill Clinton, and most recently, Barack Obama.

The inn opened in 1913 and was the architectural vision of two men: E. W. Grove, who made his money selling an elixir called Grove's Tasteless Chill Tonic, and Grove's son-in-law Fred Seely. Grove found Asheville to be good for his health, and the area inspired him to build a restful and rejuvenating inn. It took more than 400 men 12 months to build the inn, during which time they dragged hundreds of tons of boulders up the mountain using mules, rope, and pulleys. The inn is warm and welcoming, and it blends into the natural surroundings. As my husband, son, and I drove up to the entrance of the hotel, I fell in love instantly with the Old World charm of the stone buildings and rocking chairs waiting out front to greet guests.

We entered the Great Hall, which is more than 120 feet long, with ceilings soaring over 24 feet high. At one end of the Great Hall are doors leading out to the Sunset Terrace with spectacular views of Asheville and the Blue Ridge Mountains. Two enormous 14-foot-tall fireplaces in the Great Hall immediately drew our attention.

At check-in we were given our keys and, to our surprise, we were directed to the elevator attendant standing by the fireplace. My husband and I looked at each other, both thinking the same thing—elevator operator by the fireplace? We approached him and asked him to direct us to the elevator. Like something out of a Harry Potter movie, he led us to a door located in the fireplace. The elevators are hidden inside the chimneys of the stone fireplace! The operator rode with us, pushing the gate closed and working the elevator up to our floor.

The elevator door opened to our floor, and we stepped off into the Main Inn, entering an area called the Palm Court Pavilion. It was a nice open space to lounge with chairs and tables set with reading lamps. The decor made me feel like I was stepping back into the Roaring Twenties.

We were tired after traveling across the state of North Carolina. We settled in that evening to sleep, and I was awoken about an hour later by my son's coughing. In his childhood, he suffered from breathing problems, and he was experiencing some difficulty that evening. I gave him his medicine, and we sat up together for a while. He still wasn't feeling better and the room felt a little stuffy, so I threw on my robe and took him to sit out in the Palm Court area. The air was lighter there than in our room, and I took a book to read to him to calm him down while we waited for the medicine to kick in and help his breathing. We sat side by side and were relaxing and talking, and I was stroking his head and speaking softly to him.

It was close to midnight, and the inn was dead quiet. I felt a sudden chill in the air and pulled my robe tighter around me. My son also felt the chill, and he snuggled in closer to warm up. A few moments later, I felt someone around us, and as I looked up from speaking to my son, I saw the ghostly image of a woman standing next to us. Not wanting to alarm my son, I remained quiet, observing her to see what she would do next.

At the time, my son looked up as well and saw the woman too. It wasn't alarming to either of us, as her energy felt compassionate and sympathetic. She stood next to my son and seemed concerned for him and reached out her hand as if she meant to stroke his hair along with me. She was with us for a few moments and then disappeared from our view.

My son and I looked at each other with wide eyes and smiled. It wasn't the first time that we had seen a ghost; we had experienced several paranormal events together in a haunted house where we had once lived in Florida. We headed back to our hotel room, where my son jumped up on the bed to wake his dad and tell him the story. My husband couldn't believe he had missed it all. He was surprised that he had slept through everything, but that's what the fresh mountain air does for you—relaxes you into a deep sleep.

My son was still not feeling well, so we packed up and left early to get him back home. As we were checking out, I asked the people at the front desk if they had ever heard any reports of a ghost at the inn. They asked me why, and I explained what had happened with my son and me in the Palm Court. The front desk clerks crowded around to hear my story. They told me that I had seen the ghost of the Pink Lady, as she is known at the inn.

The legend of the Pink Lady states that in the 1920s, she fell or was pushed from the hallway outside her room over the railing, where she fell to the floor of the Palm Court Pavilion below. The room that she stayed in was 545, and there have been reports from people who stayed in the room of experiencing cold spots there and sometimes seeing her apparition.

Some paranormal investigators might think that the Pink Lady is a time-loop energy-imprint apparition, replaying her death over and over in the Palm Court, but that is not what we experienced. When she appeared to my son and me, she was engaged with us in the present moment, and she was aware that my son was not feeling well. She stood by wanting to comfort him in a motherly way, just as I was doing.

The front desk employees told us that a few years prior to our visit, a doctor had stayed at the hotel and reported seeing

View of the balcony where the Pink Lady is reported to have fallen to her death in the Palm Court below *(Photo by Kala Ambrose)*

her and that he had also reported that she seemed very welcoming to children.

Since that visit in 1998, we have returned to visit the Grove Park Inn many times. We've celebrated Christmas at the Grove Park Inn, as well as Thanksgiving and Easter. We've also visited many times to enjoy the inn's new spa, and I've been there for girlfriend getaways and romantic weekends with my husband and have wonderful memories with family and friends. However, we never stayed again in the Main Inn, preferring the wings and sometimes the Club Floor.

But each time we visit we do hop on the elevator with our friends and spend some time in the Palm Court in the late evenings, hoping that the Pink Lady will visit us again.

I traveled again this past year to the Grove Park Inn to conduct further research for this book on the Pink Lady, as well as to research any other paranormal activity in the hotel. I brought a video camera along in case she decided to visit with me. I didn't see her during my visit and have come to the conclusion that she is really drawn to young children. I've never slept in her room on the fifth floor, but have heard from employees at the inn that many guests report feeing her presence in the room and are often awoken by her in the evening.

While investigating paranormal activity at the Grove Park Inn, I heard some other interesting stories from the employees about the hotel's nightclub, called Elaine's. It is said to be the most haunted spot in the hotel. We've been to Elaine's Dueling Piano Bar during several of our visits, and it's always a very entertaining way to spend the evening. I've never seen a ghost or any sign of paranormal activity while there, but the employees report that the activity usually happens when Elaine's is quiet and they are cleaning up the day after a long party the evening before in the club. Music is often heard playing inside Elaine's club when no one is inside. Several ghostly apparitions have been reported to appear on the dance floor by the employees. They appear to be attending a party from decades ago, as they are dressed in attire from the 1920s and the music heard also appears to be from that time. Photographs taken at Elaine's often show a large variety of orbs in photos, as the ghostly guests appear to enjoy being around the alcohol, the music, and the lively atmosphere.

A local TV station was once located in the building next to the Grove Park Inn, and it is said that a ghost would often interfere with the equipment and enjoyed playing pranks on the staff. Some believe that the ghost is Alice, a servant who haunts the building, which originally was the Battle Mansion owned by Dr. Samuel Battle. Others believe that the ghost was the Pink Lady from the Grove Park, who enjoyed visiting the grounds and nearby home. The ghost of Dr. Battle was also seen on occasion at the TV station. The TV station has since moved out of the Battle Mansion, and the building was later demolished.

The Grove Park Inn is a beautiful, warm, and welcoming place to stay. I'm surprised that it doesn't have more ghosts that check in and never want to leave.

THE LEGENDARY BROWN MOUNTAIN LIGHTS

In the mountains of North Carolina, ghost stories and other paranormal occurrences are plentiful. The Brown Mountain Lights have been reported as ghosts rising from the ground, aliens landing on the mountain, and demons flying through the night. Little is known about the true nature of these lights. What is known is that they occur often and remain an unsolved mystery to all who have observed and studied the paranormal activity.

Brown Mountain is located in the ancient Pisgah Forest on the border of Burke and Caldwell Counties. Cherokee and Catawba Indigenous tribes shared reports on seeing the lights over Brown Mountain, as did Scots-Irish settlers and soldiers during the Civil War. Over the years, so many reports were documented that the U.S. government conducted several investigations with the U.S. Geological Department to determine the cause of the lights appearing over the mountain. To date, no conclusive evidence on what the lights are or what could cause them has been released. Basic theories like swamp gas have been ruled out at this point. Some scientists theorized that automobile lights shining from distant roads were the cause, but that theory was quickly discounted as the lights have been viewed and reported in the same way for hundreds of years, before electricity or the automobile were invented.

Locals state that on most any clear night, if one is patient enough to spend time in the vicinity of Brown Mountain, the lights can be seen. Interested locals, tourists, and paranormal researchers are often found gathered in small groups around the area hoping to see the lights as evening approaches. The best place to see them is on the Blue Ridge Parkway near mile post 302. The lights appear in clusters and will flash for a minute or so and then disappear and reappear again.

THE LEGENDARY BROWN MOUNTAIN LIGHTS (CONTINUED)

What I found incredibly interesting about the Brown Mountain Lights beyond their unexplained occurrence is that the people who have seen them have varied descriptions as to how the lights move. Some describe them as moving quickly, bouncing from place to place, while others report seeing them hovering in one space for the full time.

CHAPTER 21

ASHEVILLE

THE JUXTAPOSITION OF ASHEVILLE, FROM HEALING RESORTS AND ENDLESS VIEWS TO THE MASS MURDERER OF ASHEVILLE AND THE HAUNTED GALLOWS TRAIL

Barley's Tavern in Asheville

The city of Asheville has a unique perspective on life; its slogan is "Altitude Affects Attitude." I can't argue with this logic, as every time I travel to the Blue Ridge Mountains, I start oohing and aahing as soon as I catch my first glimpse of the mountains. I dare anyone to say they are not touched by the beauty of the area while driving to Asheville through the Pisgah Forest.

The Cherokee were the first recorded people to live on this land. They called it "The Land of the Blue Smoke," giving us the modern names of the Blue Ridge Mountains and the Great Smoky Mountains; the "smoke" is a blue haze that hangs over the mountain range.

Daniel Boone and Davy Crockett both spent time in Asheville, though at the time, it was a quiet place to pass through. Beginning in the 1880s, two events brought a surge of energy to the area. The first was the railroad, which allowed settlers and visitors to arrive comfortably in the city, and the second was Asheville's growing reputation as a healing place.

Asheville's popularity grew with its reputation for fresh mountain air and restorative properties. As a result, George Vanderbilt purchased more than 120,000 acres of land on which to build his famous Biltmore Estate.

But Asheville has not always been a recuperative, peaceful place. In the late 1700s, the Cherokee people were driven from this land in the infamous Trail of Tears. Asheville was also touched by the Civil War; it served as a gathering place for Confederate troops to regroup, heal, and gather supplies and reinforcements. The local regiment, known as the Buncombe Rifles, carried a flag made from silk dresses donated by the society women of Asheville.

The city struggled during the Great Depression, having one of the highest debt levels for a city of its size at the time when the stock market crashed. One of the reasons that residents and visitors can enjoy the beautiful architecture in downtown Asheville is that the city made a commitment to pay its debt on buildings rather than allowing them to be foreclosed during the Great Depression. This determination saved many of these buildings that might otherwise have been closed and left to fall into a state of disrepair.

Most everyone who has visited the Asheville area has also reaped the benefits of a project that began during the Depression in order to stimulate the economy. Created by Franklin Roosevelt, the Great Smoky Mountains National Park was established, and a road was built connecting North Carolina and Tennessee. We've driven this spectacular drive many times through the mountains, arriving on the other side in Gatlinburg, Tennessee. If you have the opportunity to do so, it's a drive that you and your family will never forget. The views are showstopping, and if you like driving on curving, winding roads, you'll enjoy the experience.

Asheville is a place of exploration for the body, mind, and spirit. Cradled by mountains and rivers, the powerful energy radiating from the mountains creates a unique space in which to spend some time. For some, this turns into a lifetime. Just when I think I can't see anything more striking than the mountains and sky, the city then delights me with a dazzling array of Art Deco–style buildings downtown.

Asheville has its share of haunted history, a part of that history being a haunted street and taproom near the site of the largest mass murder in the city. The taproom is called Barley's Tavern and it is located near where the old town gallows once stood. From the early 1900s, people have reported paranormal activity in this part of the city. One sighting is of a man dressed all in black that walks along the street and then, as he attempts to enter through the front door of the tavern, disappears into thin air. Locals believe that he may be the ghost of the former town executioner. Strange screams and moaning sounds are often heard around this area at night. When helpful people passing by the area hear the screams and investigate, they find no one there, only the haunting sound of a scream dissipating into the night.

It's very possible that the man in black and the screams are imprints recorded from previous events. The long history of deaths on the gallows creates an atmosphere of traumatic energy that can be felt and heard by some to this day. Whatever trauma was experienced in this area with the gallows, the energy has only intensified due to the killing of five people viciously gunned down in cold blood on one dark night in the city. I must warn you that this story is the most graphic and violent of all of the ghost stories presented here in this book, so fair warning.

In 1906, the patrons of the various taverns in this area witnessed the most horrific mass murder ever seen in the city of Asheville. According to the local legend and reports, the murderer was William Harris, a convict who had escaped from a correctional center and arrived in Asheville looking for a woman named Molly whom he called his girlfriend. He found Molly's sister Pearl in a local café and asked her where he could find Molly. Molly had never liked Will and certainly didn't think of him as her boyfriend, and she had told Pearl that if he ever came looking for her to tell him that she had moved away. Pearl told Will that Molly had moved away, and he left the café in a bitter mood. While Pearl continued dining with friends, Will Harris went on a dark and angry shopping spree. He reportedly bought a bottle of whiskey, a new suit, and a rifle from a local pawnshop owned by a man named Harry. It's unclear how Will had the money to purchase these items. Given that he had just escaped from jail, it's easy to assume he undertook some type of criminal activity along his way to Asheville to have money on him.

Dressed in his new suit, Will waited near the café and followed Pearl as she made her way back to her home near Eagle Street. After she entered her home, there was a knock on the door and Pearl, thinking it was her boyfriend, opened the door to find Will Harris standing there. He pushed his way inside, showed Pearl the gun, and demanded to know where Molly was. A few moments later, Pearl's boyfriend opened the front door and, seeing Will sitting there with a gun on Pearl, shut the door and took off running for help. Pearl's boyfriend returned shortly with two police officers. One of the police officers knocked on the door and announced, "Police!" Will responded by aiming his rifle and shooting through Pearl's front door, killing the officer. Will then kicked through the door and shot the other police officer, wounding him in the arm.

Furious, Will headed out into the street on an alcohol- and rage-fueled rampage in the city. Will began shooting at people in the streets of downtown Asheville, and some reports state that he was screaming at the time that he was the devil and at other times shouting that he was from hell and was going back and taking as many people as he could with him.

Hearing the gunshots and shouting in the street, the legends state that a man named Benjamin stepped out of his shop on Eagle Street to investigate. Benjamin had just enough time to see Will before Will took aim and shot Benjamin in the head.

Will moved on toward the area that is now known as Biltmore Avenue. A man walking in the area stepped out from the alleyway to cross the street, and without hesitation, Will shot and killed him on the spot.

Near the corner of Eagle Street, a group of men stood chatting close to the road. The men saw Will coming up the street with the rifle, and they took off running, all except for one man named Tom, who thought the group was playing a practical joke on him. Tom stood and faced Will, and Will shot Tom, making him victim number four. Will could not find the other men who had been standing there with Tom; it was later reported that they were hiding under a nearby porch and witnessed the altercation.

Meanwhile, the wounded police officer gathered reinforcements, including Officer Bailey, who used a wooden telephone pole as cover while shooting at Will. The officer missed, and Harris shot through the telephone pole. The bullet entered and passed through the mouth of the officer, killing him instantly. The bullet then continued across the street, breaking a window in a store and lodging in the wall of the shop.

At this point in his rampage, Will had shot at many people and killed five people and a dog. Finished with his shooting spree, Will fled to hide. The town of Asheville was in an uproar, and police and a town posse gathered to search for the gunman. A reward was set for his capture. Reportedly Harry, the pawnshop owner, was so upset that he had sold this rifle to Will Harris that he opened up his pawnshop and loaned guns to the posse to go hunt for Will.

Will was found by the posse two days later hiding under some bushes in the nearby town of Fletcher. The group of men called out for Will to give himself up, and Will shot into the crowd. At this point the posse opened fire, and it is reported that Will Harris was shot more than 100 times by the men who found him.

As horrible as this story is, here's where the tale becomes even more eerie. The group of men threw his body on a wagon and delivered the corpse of Will Harris to the undertakers in Asheville. As was the custom in many places back at this time, Will Harris's body was put on display for the public to view. So many people wanted to see the body that it was reportedly moved outside so that the public wouldn't have to wait in long lines. Reportedly thousands of people from miles around came to view his corpse. The public display ended when people began to express their rage by walking up and shooting the corpse. At this point, police had to intervene and shut things down. Interestingly, no one knows what happened to the body of Will Harris at this point. There appears to be no burial record filed. Some people surmise that his body was sold to a traveling carnival, as this was popular during this time, to display the body of criminals who had done particularly vicious crimes.

The town of Asheville suffered tremendously during this time, grieving for their lost citizens and the fear that had overtaken the town on that night. For months afterward, people would report seeing and hearing the dead in this area, saying they would see the bodies writhing in pain in the street as the men died and blood poured out from them into the street.

Others would hear gunshots, shouts, and screams that sounded as real as the night they occurred.

This area had already been witness to many deaths and negative energy with the old town gallows nearby. Spirits were often seen walking along the streets late at night. These stories were often discounted, as this area of the city had a large number of taverns and other drinking establishments and it was shrugged off as another type of spirit having an affect on the person who shared an experience.

After the event with Will Harris, the sightings began to grow in number, and dark forms were seen standing near the area where the apparition would appear as if they were watching the event as well. These dark forms would then hover around the area, as if they were soaking up the residual negative energy from the event. Some people began describing them as shadow people. Many people also report that when they are in this area late at night, they see the ghost of an undertaker carrying a body away into the darkness.

Barley's Tavern still stands in this area. It is now known as Barley's Tap Room and Pizzeria. This in itself is part of the history of the event. Not only is Barley's in the vicinity of where the shootings took place, but the mere fact that Barley's is still operating as a tavern speaks to the history and evolution of the city. After the horrendous event with Will Harris, prohibitionists (people against the consumption of alcohol) took this opportunity to campaign for prohibition in Asheville. Their argument was based on the fact that had Will Harris not been drinking, he would not have lost his senses and gone on an alcohol-fueled killing rampage. In the midst of the city's grief, their argument was successful, and in 1907, Asheville became the first town in the state of North Carolina to vote down alcohol and to close saloons and liquor distilleries. Prohibition became law in the United States in 1920 and was repealed in 1933. Prohibition led to people using fast cars to haul moonshine and bootleg liquor through the mountains of North Carolina to paying customers. For NASCAR fans, this is how their sport began.

Asheville now has more "spirits" than other areas of the country. The city now boasts more microbreweries per capita than most other cities in the United States, including Portland, Oregon. The city also hosts the Brewgrass Festival each year.

My husband and I visited Barley's Tavern to enjoy some spirits now that they're legal again, while talking about spirits and the ghosts in the area. We chatted with employees and locals at the bar to learn more about the story. Not only did we learn about the shooting rampage of Will Harris, but we also learned that Barley's also has reports of haunted activity, and a ghost is often felt in the building. Most believe it's a woman, as they smell perfume when she comes around. Perhaps she's been at Barley's long before Will Harris appeared on the scene, or maybe she came later and just enjoys the company and activity at the tavern. At one point in its history, the building served as an appliance store; maybe the female ghost is still shopping for the right appliance.

Inside Barley's where the woman ghost has often been seen

Some locals report seeing the dark shadow of a ghost man walking along the street near the tavern. The man never appears to enter the tavern, nor is he seen inside the building; he is only seen walking in the area. Some have reported seeing him appear and then a few moments later, hearing a bloodcurdling scream. Each person that we spoke with who had seen this man said that his presence was terrifying and that they could feel a sense of cold and dread washing over them.

While visiting the taproom and the surrounding area, we didn't experience any paranormal activity, but we enjoyed ourselves tremendously. Barley's is a lively place, with music and a vibrant mix of locals and visitors to the city. Our brief visit there was not enough to detect haunted activity. See for yourself if the area is haunted by visiting Barley's Tavern on a moonlit night, but don't go alone; be sure to bring several friends with you.

THE INMATES OF THE GREAT SMOKY MOUNTAINS RAILROAD TUNNEL, DILLSBORO

When the Great Smoky Mountains Railroad brought the railroad to the mountains of North Carolina, it became so popular that six passenger trains were running every day between Asheville and Lake Junaluska in the early 1900s. Plans were made to expand the railroad farther into the mountains, which was a daunting task at best. In order to expand the railways, an 836-foot tunnel needed to be built near the town of Dillsboro through the Balsam Mountains at an elevation of more than 3,000 feet.

Not surprisingly, the railroad was experiencing great difficulty finding men who were willing to do the work on this project. The company made the decision to have convicts brought in to dig out the tunnel and lay the rails. The convicts were trucked into the area in shackles and watched over by armed guards throughout the project.

In order to get the convicts to the area where they needed to dig, they had to cross over the Tuckasegee River. The guards used rafts to bring 20 men at a time across the river to work in the tunnel. One day one of the rafts capsized, tossing the guard and the 20 inmates into the water. The inmates were shackled together, and within minutes 19 of the 20 inmates drowned.

The armed guard, Fleet Foster, was rescued from drowning by the one convict who survived. The convict's name was Anderson Drake. Drake survived by sheer luck, as his shackles had broken free during the fray, allowing him to swim to shore. As he swam, he noticed that Foster was drowning and so he pulled Foster to shore, saving his life. Once the two men were safely on shore, Foster stated that he believed that during the process of Drake saving his life, that Drake had stolen

Foster's wallet. Drake was whipped and beaten by the guards and immediately put to work in the tunnel.

The 19 inmates who drowned that day were pulled from the river and buried in unmarked graves on top of a small hill near the mouth of the tunnel. Witnesses report that ghosts appear in the tunnel to this day and that the sounds of men crying for help and chains rattling can be heard around the tunnel.

An interesting side note about this tunnel is that it was used in the filming of the movie *The Fugitive,* in which Harrison Ford played the leading role.

THE MYSTERIOUS VORTEX OF MYSTERY HILL, BLOWING ROCK

Along your journey of strange, mysterious, and unexplainable sites in haunted North Carolina, Mystery Hill should be on your list of places to check out and explore. The main attraction at Mystery Hill is the Mystery House, where there is a gravitational anomaly. As you enter the Mystery House, your body begins to lean at a 45-degree angle from the gravitational pull. The laws of physics work differently here, and the guides will show you a variety of examples, including watching water and a ball move uphill. Their exhibits and interactive displays in the Hall of Mystery also include the Spooky Spigot, the Magic Light Bulb, Hologram, and the Flying Mirror. It's also just plain fun to try and stand upright while your body fights to lean at a 45-degree angle.

The explanation for the anomalies at the Mystery Hill is a vortex. A vortex is a pull of force that moves in a spiral pattern and appears on earth in electric, magnetic, or electromagnetic forms. Scientific examples of this force include the funnel formed by a tornado, the circular pattern and eye formed in a hurricane, or the motion of our solar system revolving around the sun. In metaphysical terms, vortices are said to be formed not only by natural occurrences as seen in storms, but also by people and beings who understand how to open portals to the other realms and spiritual planes. There are also energy center vortices along the chakra lines of the earth, and certain sacred sites are built on these lines, which are called ley lines. The most well known examples are the Great Pyramid in Egypt and Stonehenge in England. Other natural areas display strong vortex energy, such as Sedona, Arizona, and Mount Shasta in California. Mystery Hill displays

many of the anomalies that can be observed in an area with a vortex, including having two people stand on a level platform to see how perspective changes in a vortex. As a person walks closer to magnetic north, they appear to be shorter, and as they move toward magnetic south, they appear taller in height. Were you to observe the person standing in either of these spots, you would swear that they are taller or shorter depending upon their location; the effect is eerie when they leave the spot and stand in front of you. All in all, it's a fun adventure to experience the vortex firsthand.

The sign to Blowing Rock showcases the legend and lore.

CHAPTER 22

BLOWING ROCK

THE LEGEND OF BLOWING ROCK AND THE GREEN PARK INN

The little town of Blowing Rock is a picturesque place surrounded by mountains, green forest, and waterfalls. It gets my vote for the most romantic town in North Carolina, with its own native Romeo and Juliet love story. It was once the home of the Cherokee and Catawba tribes, who got along as well as the Capulets and Montagues did.

Blowing Rock was named after two natural occurrences in the area, one being the high winds that blow around the mountains, which can be downright chilling in the winter and a cool respite in the summer. This accounts for the town's population swelling by the thousands each summer, as tourists from other southern states flock to the area to enjoy the cooler weather.

The second reason for the town's name of Blowing Rock is a rock formation in the area that stretches out more than 1,500 feet above the John's River gorge. As the high wind gusts blow around this substantial rock face, the current swirls around the shape of the rock, causing objects to blow upward around it.

The naming of the town begins with the Native American legend, which starts out like so many of these stories do: with a sweet, romantic tale. There once was a boy who met a girl, and they fell in love. One was from the Cherokee tribe and the other from the Catawba tribe. (Some say that it was the Chickasaw tribe, not Catawba.) The two tribes did not get along, and so their innocent love was forbidden.

To hide their love from their families and tribes, they often met at the rock formation to be together in secret. Here they would pass the time and dream of the day that their families would make peace so they could marry and begin their life together.

One day, the young man met his love at the rock and told her that his tribe had informed him that he would need to prepare to go to war tomorrow against her tribe. They were both very upset, and the legend states that she begged him to run away with her so they could be together. The young man was torn between his love for the young woman and his allegiance to his tribe. He became so upset that he decided that rather than make a choice between family and his love, he would end his life instead.

Blowing Rock and the beautiful Blue Ridge Mountains, where the young man was said to have returned to his lover's arms

He stood up and jumped off the rock, in a free fall to the gorge far below. In a panic, the young woman called out to the Great Spirit to save him as he fell. The Great Spirit, hearing the young woman's call and feeling the love between the young lovers, felt compassion for their plight. The Great Spirit blew a huge gust of wind around the rock, which stopped her lover from falling and then lifted his body in the air, returning him back into her arms where she stood on the rock. Overcome with this gift of life, it is assumed then that the two lovers left the area and their families to be together. The legend ends here, but the name of this area became known as Blowing Rock, and lovers visit this spot from around the world, caught up in the romantic tale.

Some people say that if you sit quietly, you can hear voices carried in the wind from the ancestors of the natives who once lived here and, if you're really lucky, the Great Spirit may share a message in the wind with you as you visit.

In the mid-18th century, the population of Blowing Rock expanded as Scottish and Irish settlers began to move into the area. One of the families who settled in Blowing Rock was the Greene family, who built their home on the site where the Green Park Inn is now located.

The village of Blowing Rock incorporated in 1889 with a population of around 300 people. Tourism was already a primary source of revenue at this time, as southern families traveled to the location to camp and rent rooms at boarding homes in order to escape the high summer temperatures.

This thriving business prompted the opening of the Green Park Hotel in 1891, which is located 3,600 feet above sea level in the Blue Ridge Mountains along the Eastern Continental Divide. As tourism boomed, several other hotels in the village also opened during this time, including the Watauga Hotel and the Mayview Manor. The Watauga Hotel burned down twice. After the second time, the owners believed that it was cursed and did not rebuild.

The Mayview Manor lasted longer, until around 1966, before it closed. It sat in a state of disrepair for 12 years before being demolished. Many local residents expressed their remorse that the manor was not purchased by the city or a developer interested in restoring the historic property.

The Green Park Inn has stood the test of time as the only remaining inn of those three. It has a history of famous guests, including Herbert Hoover, Eleanor Roosevelt, Margaret Mitchell, Calvin Coolidge, John D. Rockefeller, and Annie Oakley. The inn also has a long history of haunted activity.

In its heyday, people stayed at the inn for months at a time. At one time the inn had its own post office, zip code, hairdresser, and doctor on-site. As charming and romantic as Blowing Rock is, there are also sad tales of romance gone wrong.

Guests and employees of the Green Park Inn have recorded a number of strange disturbances and paranormal events at the hotel. Some reports state that Room 318 is the most haunted room in the hotel, where a young woman reportedly died in the room decades ago. There doesn't appear to have been an autopsy, but legends state that she is believed to have died from a broken heart or by committing suicide. Apparently, she waited at the church for her groom to arrive for their wedding, but he never did. She retreated to this room in despair and passed away soon after.

In the same room, the scent of pipe smoke is also detected on occasion. Theories include that the groom might have come to the inn to find her and apologize, only to find her dead, and that his spirit has now joined hers at the inn. Others feel that a more sinister male spirit haunts the inn. They report feeling cold spots a few moments before detecting his pipe smoke as he searches for the female ghost.

Many of the reports of paranormal activity appear to originate in several of the rooms on the third floor. Some reports state that the old caretaker of the inn, who many years ago looked after the place when it would close for the winter months, stayed in Room 327. Many claim that, though he passed on many years back, he remains at the inn in spirit. Some guests have reported the feeling of a man watching them in the room and hearing noises and movement like someone walking in the room while they sleep. The caretaker seems to stay in this room and feels as comfortable living there today in the afterlife as he did while alive.

While the ghosts of the third floor all appear to be a bit lonely and searching for something in the afterlife, the ghosts of the second floor reported by guests seem to be enjoying their time at the inn. Most of the second-floor ghost experiences shared by guests are stories of hearing children running noisily back and forth through the halls, laughing and playing. When the guests open their door to see the children, the hallway is always found to be completely empty.

So many paranormal incidents have been reported over the years that in 2004, a ghost register was installed at the reception desk. This register allowed all guests who experienced seeing a ghost or other supernatural activity to record their experiences. A number of North Carolina paranormal investigators have also stayed at the inn to investigate the haunted activity. Several have also held conferences on the paranormal at the inn.

The hotel closed in 2010 and was put up on auction. It was purchased by new owners and underwent renovation the same year. Reportedly, a large amount of the original furnishings were sold during this time. The hotel reopened in 2011.

I toured Blowing Rock and the Green Park Inn while conducting research in the area but did not stay in one of the haunted rooms. During my stay in the area, the inn was in a state of disrepair, undergoing renovation, so my husband and I decided to stay elsewhere for the evening. I hope to return to see the inn again in the future, this time to stay overnight, as I'm curious to experience any paranormal activity that may be present, as well as to see if the renovations and removal of furniture have had any effect on the amount of paranormal activity in the inn. Many times renovations stir up ghosts along with the dust, as they often don't care for the change in their surroundings. Ghosts are also known to attach themselves to furniture and other belongings, and it's possible that some of them have followed the sold items to new homes around the country.

It's always a pleasure to see a historic site being lovingly restored and cared for as part of our nation's and state's heritage. A visit to Blowing Rock will be back on my to-do list soon, as I always enjoy my time there. Blowing Rock is a peaceful community with romance and spirits literally blowing in the air.

MASS MURDERER CHARLIE LAWSON, GERMANTON

On December 25, 1929, tobacco farmer Charlie Lawson, in Germanton, North Carolina, shot and bludgeoned his entire family, which included his wife, Fannie, and six of his seven children. His oldest son, Arthur, age 18, was not home at the time. The other children were Marie, 17; Carrie, 12; Maybell, 7; James, 4; Raymond, 2; and Marylou, 4 months.

At the time, no one was sure why Charlie killed his entire family. A few days prior to the mass murder, he had taken his family to town to buy them all new clothes and had a family portrait taken. These clothes later became their burial outfits, and the family portrait was printed in newspapers around the country when the murder was reported.

In 1990, M. Bruce Jones and Trudy J. Smith published the book *White Christmas, Bloody Christmas,* which contained interviews and information from the extended family about the murders. Trudy J. Smith also wrote a second book on the topic, *The Meaning of Our Tears,* which delved further into the family history.

The legend around this story is that Charlie's wife had confided to her sisters-in-law and aunts that she believed Charlie was committing incest with their oldest daughter, Marie. She also believed that Marie was now pregnant with his child. A friend of Marie's also shared that Marie had told her that she was pregnant with her father's child.

The theories and opinions differ according to the various family descendants.

After the murders, Charlie's brother Marion Lawson opened the house as a tourist attraction for many years. The mass murder in North Carolina has continued to shock and sadden all who hear the story. Not only have books been written about it, but the tragedy also prompted the Stanley Brothers in 1956 to record a folk song written

MASS MURDERER CHARLIE LAWSON, GERMANTON (CONTINUED)

about the event, titled "The Murder of the Lawson Family." A documentary titled *A Christmas Family Tragedy* has also been created, and the producers donate 10% of the proceeds from the film to domestic violence prevention charities.

The Lawson house was torn down in 1984, and reportedly the wood for the home was used to build a nearby covered bridge. The ghosts of the family are still reportedly seen around the gravesites of Charlie Lawson and his family in Browder Cemetery in Germanton.

CHAPTER 23

CHARLOTTE

THE HAUNTING CHARM OF CHARLOTTE'S FOURTH WARD AND THE OLD SETTLER'S CEMETERY

Located in the historic Fourth Ward section of downtown Charlotte, the Old Settler's Cemetery is the oldest cemetery in the city. The area is easy to walk around, and a tourist information office on South Tryon provides maps of a self-guided tour so that you can see other historic sites along the way to the cemetery. The residential district is laid out in one of the easiest patterns I've ever found to get around a city, as the historic center of Charlotte is divided into four wards and the Square, at the intersection of Trade and Tryon, represents the center point.

I have visited Charlotte many times, including bringing my mystery school students to see the Dead Sea Scrolls exhibit at Discovery Place. During that visit, we stayed at the historic Dunhill Hotel, which is right in the heart of the city and all of its activities, including nearby Spirit Square. The Dunhill is a beautifully restored hotel that opened in 1929 and was originally called the Mayfair Manor apartment hotel. Many of the rooms were rented on a long-term basis, which was common at that time.

At the Dunhill Hotel, the European style with neoclassic touches had me feeling right at home, and I could easily imagine living at that hotel. For all that we wanted to do and see in Charlotte, it was perfectly located. We could walk to see

The Old Settler's Cemetery in Charlotte

the Dead Sea Scrolls exhibit and enjoy nearby restaurants and entertainment. Some of us even hopped in a carriage ride one evening to tour downtown.

After we wrapped up our tour of the Dead Sea Scrolls, we returned to the Dunhill to freshen up and prepare to go to dinner as a group. Two of my students were ready very quickly, so they decided to go down to wait in the lobby for the rest of us. There is a piano in the lobby with live music in the late afternoon and early evening, and my students decided to wait in this area and enjoy the music. As they stood there chatting, they noticed a ghostly figure standing by the piano, evidently enjoying the music. Neither of them had ever seen a ghost before, and it was a big surprise for both of them.

By the time I arrived downstairs, the ghost was gone. When we had checked in, I felt the presence of a female ghost in our room. She was shy and unassuming. I didn't know if she was the same ghost at the piano or not, but our descriptions of what we both saw and felt were similar. Whoever she is, she's very pleasant. She appears to be enjoying her stay and the music at the hotel, like any other guest.

During another visit to Charlotte, we returned to the Fourth Ward to eat at a pub many locals had suggested we try for the food, the atmosphere, and the haunted history. It is Alexander Michael's, or, as I was told by another diner, it's often called Al Mike's. Al Mike's opened in 1983 in a historic location in the Fourth Ward. The building first opened as a grocery store in 1897 and continued to operate as a store through 1960. Old-timers know the history and refer to it as the Crowell-Berryhill place. The original owner was Wilson Crowell, who ran the Star Mill grocery, and later Ernest Berryhill began running Berryhill grocery here beginning in 1907. The building continued to metamorphose, operating as a laundromat from 1960 to 1973 and then as Mac Mac's Deli until Al Mike's opened in 1983. There are reports by the locals of a friendly ghost that sits at the pub, enjoying the atmosphere and most likely hoping someone will take his order. What's unclear is when the ghost first attached himself to the location.

Pubs, bars, and restaurants are popular sites frequented by ghosts. Some stay because they enjoyed alcohol so much during their physical life that they enjoy just being around it in the afterlife. Some theories on the matter state that if the ghost can gather close enough around a person who has been drinking, they can experience the same sensation in their spirit form. For a ghost who enjoyed drinking, this is a contact high, and it's rare for them to want to leave a pub that they enjoyed. This is often also the case with cigar and pipe smoking. Many ghosts still carry with them the scent of tobacco that they loved so much when alive. Other ghosts are often detected by the scent of a favorite perfume they wore throughout their lifetime.

Also located in this area of Charlotte is the aptly named Spirit Square, which has its haunted history centered around the Loonis McGlohon Theatre. The theatre is currently closed, but a few of the locals were happy to share ghost stories they had heard about it.

Spirit Square was built in 1909 as the site of the First Baptist Church. In 1970, the church moved to a new building and the city created a community center here focusing on the arts and community theater, renaming the area Spirit Square. The original Baptist Church sanctuary became the home of the McGlohon Theatre, named after the legendary Charlotte jazz pianist and composer Loonis McGlohon.

The legends and lore state that workers frequently reported hearing a young girl singing in the theatre when it was empty while they were inside cleaning and making repairs. It would be easy to discount this as someone practicing in a different part of the theatre, but when the workers investigated, they found the place to be empty. The songs as well were not from current performances but were old church hymns. It appears that the ghost had been there since the early days when the theatre was the Baptist Church. Employees have also reported that they hear people walking around the empty theatre.

As I continued on my walk, I headed toward my reason for this investigative visit. This time I had traveled to Charlotte to check out another historic site in the Fourth Ward, the Old Settler's Cemetery. The Old Settler's Cemetery is so well-kept and peaceful that it feels like you're in a park. You'll often see people having their lunch in the cemetery, as well as walking their dogs or just hanging out and enjoying the day. The cemetery was the first municipal burying ground in Charlotte and was established in 1776. The cemetery continued to operate until 1867, when it was closed by the city. Several burials were conducted in the cemetery through 1884 with special permission.

Reportedly, the Old Settler's Cemetery is the burial ground for some of the most prominent citizens of the city of Charlotte and surrounding Mecklenburg County from the late 18th and early 19th centuries. The oldest known grave is of Joel Baldwin, who was buried October 21, 1776. Some of the most notable residents of the city buried in the Old Settler's Cemetery include Thomas Polk, who founded the town and served as a Revolutionary War officer; U.S. Congressman Greene Washington Caldwell; U.S. Congressman William Davidson; Major General George Graham, best known for holding back General Cornwallis's troops at McIntire's Farm during the Revolutionary War; and Dr. Nathaniel Alexander, a former governor of North Carolina and a surgeon.

There are many interesting stories about some of the people buried in the cemetery. The one that I enjoyed most was about Maj. Gen. George Graham. He was part of the Mecklenburg Patriots, who were considered by the British to be some of the most "hostile forces" in the army. In 1780, Graham and 12 other Mecklenburg Patriots fought off more than 400 British soldiers at McIntyre's Farm. This battle became known as the Battle of the Hornets due to General Cornwallis remarking about the battle, "There's a rebel behind every bush, it's a veritable nest of hornets." This amused Charlotte citizens to no end, and they decided to give Charlotte the nickname "The Hornet's Nest."

There may be even more interesting people buried here, but the cemetery is so old that some of the markers are no longer legible and it's unclear if there are records of every person who was buried here. I chatted with several people visiting the cemetery, and they shared stories they had heard of ghosts there. Some said that there are unmarked gravesites in the cemetery that hold some restless spirits that need a proper burial. Others reported seeing a war general walking on the grounds during sunset. I loved hanging out in the cemetery. It felt comfortable and even relaxing. Granted, I was there in the daytime, and a nighttime visit might prove to feel quite different, but I was not alone in my assessment of finding the cemetery to be a comfortable place to spend some time, as many local citizens were there with me doing just the same thing. As I enjoyed the day, the sunshine, and the beautiful natural setting among the trees, I chuckled at my thoughts. Basically, in a bustling city like Charlotte, we the living were haunting a cemetery in order to find some peace and quiet. How's that for an ironic turn of events?

I didn't see a ghost during my time there in the cemetery, but I did feel the "spirit" of the place, and I think all the notable people buried there are quite content with being revered and visited by the generations of people who have come over the years. Perhaps they revel in the joy that Charlotte has thrived and grown into the city that she is, and they know that their sacrifices and service helped make her the queen she is today.

THE SAD PREACHER IN THE CHAPEL OF REST, LENOIR

Sometime in the early 1920s, the preacher of the Chapel of Rest reportedly caught his wife cheating on him. Overcome with grief, he allegedly committed suicide by slitting his wrists and then hanging himself from the rafters of the church on a Saturday evening. The next morning as parishioners entered the church for Sunday services, they found their preacher hanging from the rafters, his blood spilled all along the floor.

The legend states that you can still see a bloodstain on the floor. Reportedly, it has been cleaned hundreds of times but never goes away. Witnesses claim that on certain Saturday nights, the ghostly image of the preacher can still be seen hanging from the rafters.

The chapel is open during daylight hours and is visited often by tourists and paranormal investigators. A cemetery is located behind the chapel, and EVP recordings have been captured in both the church and cemetery. The cemetery is older than the chapel, with gravesites beginning in the 1800s. The original chapel was built in 1887 and burned down completely in 1916. A new chapel was constructed that still stands today. It was acquired by the Chapel of Rest Preservation Society in 1984 and fully restored in 2002 with a breezeway and bathroom added on the property. The chapel is now listed on the National Register of Historic Places.

Most people who visit the chapel find it to be peaceful, well kept, and surrounded by a beautiful setting in the valley. Ghostly activity is found there, but most likely due to the suicide it is what is called a "residual haunting," a time-loop recording of a traumatic or highly stressful event, where the energy is so strong that it creates an imprint in the area.

THE SAD PREACHER IN THE CHAPEL OF REST, LENOIR (CONTINUED)

The prayers of the parishioners over the years and the people who continue to visit have balanced this imprint by creating a peaceful, positive energy of their making, which appears to override any residual negative energy on the property and in the building. Having said that, I wouldn't care to spend a Saturday night in the church with the unhappy ghost of the preacher.

HAUNTING THEME PARKS OF NORTH CAROLINA

The **Tweetsie Railroad** is a theme park located in Blowing Rock, North Carolina. The park offers amusement rides and a working steam locomotive that takes visitors on a 3-mile ride around the area. Launched in 1957 as a Wild West theme park, it has continued to expand and grow over the decades. One of the most popular events at Tweetsie is the Ghost Train Halloween Festival held in October. Train engineer Casey Bones and his crew take you on a haunted train ride, and there's a haunted house with 13 rooms in the park, as well as a bone yard and a "black hole." The Freaky Forest was added in 2009, and dances with ghosts and ghouls are held on Tweetsie's Main Street in the evening. There's also a Creepy Carnival and Haunted Saloon.

The **Carowinds Theme Park,** located just outside of Charlotte, is best known for two major attractions—the park boasts 12 roller coasters, and in October the park turns into "Scarowinds," releasing more than 300 monsters that wander the park scaring ghouls and guys. Haunting attractions include Corn Stalkers, Dead Inn, Slaughter House, the Asylum, the Feeding Frenzy, and the Cemetery.

GHOST-HUNTING TRAVEL GUIDE

VISITING THE HAUNTED SITES OF NORTH CAROLINA

North Carolina can be divided into three major sections: Coastal Carolina (the East Coast and the Outer Banks); the Piedmont, which includes the Triad and the Triangle area, and West Carolina (the Blue Ridge/Appalachian Mountains and surrounding foothills). This book has been divided into these three sections for ease of travel.

North Carolina was one of the 13 original colonies, settled by colonists with a small number of slave plantations along the east coast. In the 1700s, North Carolina's biggest problem was pirates along the coast. The rest of the state developed into farms, with tobacco and cotton being the largest crops. The state was largely impoverished after the Civil War and remained so through the Great Depression. The largest economic recovery for the state began with farm programs for cotton and tobacco in the 1930s.

The information included in this book was gathered during my research and writing of Ghost Hunting North Carolina, and the history is reported to the best of my knowledge. Some of the historic sites do not wish to share information regarding any haunted history or paranormal activity at their locations, and in those cases, I gathered information from locals, visitors, and employees who agreed to speak off the record. As well, throughout the book I report my personal experiences and observations as they occurred at the various sites. It still must be said, though, that in researching haunted sites, there are more legends than facts in many cases, and this book is to be taken in this regard.

I believe that there are many more haunted locations around the state of North Carolina than are currently widely known. During my travels across the state meeting with people, I found that many local residents were willing to discuss haunted activities in their local neighborhoods, including restaurants, bars, theaters, homes, and historic locations, but the owners of the sites many times refused to discuss the matter in any capacity.

I encountered this situation in several historic locations during my research. While many southern states share and often embrace the information of their haunted history, North Carolina is still in a state of flux. Younger generations are open about discussing what they've experienced and seen in regards to supernatural and paranormal experiences, while some of the older generations are not comfortable admitting that the afterlife may continue in ghost form on the earth plane.

I've encountered every kind of response during my journey with this book, including having one senior staff member at a well-known historic location respond to my question by saying to me, "When you have a legitimate question, you are welcome to return and ask it." Ouch! My "illegitimate" question, by the way, was, "Are there any stories of haunted history in this location?" Evidently for some, even daring to ask about the possibility of ghosts existing in an area is not a "legitimate" question.

By email, I queried the staff of another historic site about its haunted history, which hundreds of people have experienced. They did not respond directly to my email, but accidentally copied me as they sent my email up their chain of command, in which they asked what should be "done with me asking these questions." In the past, this location had admitted on its public tours that it had haunted activity but now was receiving pressure not to discuss the matter anymore.

The staff at yet another historic location told me that they had been warned that they would lose their nonprofit standing and funds should they discuss the haunted events ongoing at their location.

My hope is that this book, along with the interest in both history and ghosts from many of the residents and visitors to the state of North Carolina, will sway these organizations to begin to report and share the paranormal activity taking place at their haunted historic sites.

GHOSTLY RESOURCES

The information below contains the contact information for the sites mentioned in the book. As with any travel arrangements, it is always best to verify information before making travel plans to ensure that the destination is still open and accepting visitors.

EAST CAROLINA

Attmore-Oliver House
511 Broad Street
New Bern, NC 28560
252-638-8558
newbernhistorical.org/attmore-oliver-house

Beaufort Historic District
historicbeaufort.com

Bellamy Mansion
503 Market Street
Wilmington, NC 28401
910-251-3700
bellamymansion.org

Blount-Bridgers House
130 Bridgers Street
Tarboro, NC 27886
252-823-4159
visitnc.com/listing/fRur/blount-bridgers-house-hobson-pittman-memorial-gallery

Cape Hatteras Lighthouse
Off Route 12,
30 miles south of Rodanthe
N35°15'09.8" W75°31'39.8"
Buxton, NC 27920
252-995-4474
nps.gov/caha

Cedar Grove Cemetery
808 George Street
New Bern, NC 28563
252-639-7501
visitnewbern.com/things-to-do/history/cedar-grove-cemetery

Currituck Beach Lighthouse
1101 Corolla Village Road
Corolla, NC 27927
252-453-4939
currituckbeachlight.com

Fayetteville Women's Club
225 Dick Street
Fayetteville, NC 28301
910-483-6009

Fort Fisher
1610 Ft. Fisher Boulevard South
Kure Beach, NC 28449
910-251-7340
nchistoricsites.org/fisher/fisher.htm

Fort Macon
2303 East Fort Macon Road
Atlantic Beach, NC 28512
252-726-3775
ncparks.gov/state-parks/fort-macon-state-park

Foscue Plantation
7509 US 17
Pollocksville, NC 28573
252-224-1803
foscueplantation.com

Ghosts of New Bern Tour
246 Middle Street
New Bern, NC 28560
252-635-1410
hauntednewbern.com

Harvey Mansion
221 South Front Street
New Bern, NC 28560
252-635-3232

Lake Phelps
Pettigrew State Park
2252 Lake Shore Road
Creswell, NC 27928
252-797-4475
ncparks.gov/state-parks/pettigrew-state-park

Lost Colony Genealogy DNA and Archaeology Research Group
Anne Poole, Co-founder and Research Director
rootsweb.com/~molcgdrg;
the-lost-colony.blogspot.com

Lost Colony Waterside Theatre
1409 National Park Drive
Manteo, NC 27954
252-473-2127
nps.gov/places/000/waterside-theatre.htm

North Carolina Maritime Museum—Beaufort
315 Front Street
Beaufort, NC 28516
252-504-7740
ncmaritimemuseums.com

Oakdale Cemetery
520 North 15th Street
Wilmington, NC 28401
910-762-5682
oakdalecemetery.org

Old Burying Grounds
North side of Ann Street between Craven and Turner Streets
Beaufort, NC 28516
historicbeaufort.com/burygnd1.htm

Somerset Place
2572 Lake Shore Road
Creswell, NC 27928
252-379-6020
nchistoricsites.org/somerset/somerset.htm

USS North Carolina Battleship
1 Battleship Road
Wilmington, NC 28401
910-399-9100
battleshipnc.com

CENTRAL CAROLINA

Bentonville Battlefield
5466 Harper House Road
Four Oaks, NC 27524
910-594-0789
historicsites.nc.gov/all-sites/bentonville-battlefield

Cabe's Land Cemetery
6101 Cole Mill Road
Durham, NC 27705
cemeterycensus.com/nc/orng/cem103.htm

Carolina History and Haunts
Greensboro and Charlotte, NC
833-628-6277
carolinahistoryandhaunts.com

Carolina Inn
211 Pittsboro Street
Chapel Hill, NC 27516
919-933-2001
carolinainn.com

Cary Community Arts Center
101 Dry Avenue
Cary, NC 27513
919-469-4069
carync.gov/recreation-enjoyment/facilities/cary-arts-center

Chowan University
1 University Place
Murfreesboro, NC 27855
252-398-6500
chowan.edu

Devil's Tramping Ground
Bennett, NC
On private property, trespassing not allowed

Hillcrest Cemetery
608 Page Street
Cary, NC 27511
carync.gov/services-publications/historic-preservation/hillcrest-cemetery#ad-image-4

Horace Williams House
610 East Rosemary Street
Chapel Hill, NC 27514
preservationchapelhill.org/horace-williams-house

Korner's Folly
413 South Main Street
Kernersville, NC 27284
336-996-7922
kornersfolly.org

Mordecai Plantation
1 Mimosa Street
Raleigh, NC 27604
919-996-4364
raleighnc.gov/parks-and-recreation/places/mordecai-historic-park

Page-Walker Hotel
119 Ambassador Loop
Cary, NC 27512
919-460-4963
friendsofpagewalker.org

Raleigh Pub Crawl & Haunted Adventure Tour
Tobacco Road Tours
919-371-2653
tobaccoroadtours.com

Raleigh State Capitol
1 E Edenton Street
Raleigh, NC 27601
919-733-4994
nchistoricsites.org/capitol/default.htm

Rhine Research Center
2741 Campus Walk Avenue
Bldg. 500
Durham, NC 27705
919-309-4600
rhine.org

Historic Stagville
5828 Old Oxford Highway
Durham, NC 27712
919-620-0120
nchistoricsites.org/stagville/stagville.htm

Star Hotel
118 North Main Street
Star, NC 27356
910-428-2565

WEST CAROLINA

Barley's Taproom & Pizzeria
42 Biltmore Avenue
Asheville, NC 28801
828-255-0504
barleystaproom.com

Biltmore
1 Lodge Street
Asheville, NC 28803
800-411-3812
biltmore.com

Blowing Rock
432 The Rock Road
Blowing Rock, NC 28605
828-295-7111
theblowingrock.com

Brown Mountain Lights
Blue Ridge Parkway
Mile Post 310
Morganton, NC
westernncattractions.com/BMLights.htm

Carowinds/Scarowinds Theme Park
14523 Carowinds Boulevard
Charlotte, NC 28273
704-588-2600
carowinds.com

Chapel of Rest
NC Highway 268,
9 miles north of Lenoir
Lenoir, NC 28645
chapelofrest.org

Dunhill Hotel
237 North Tryon Street
Charlotte, NC 28202
704-332-4141
dunhillhotel.com

Green Park Inn
9239 Valley Boulevard
Blowing Rock, NC 28605
828-414-9230
greenparkinn.com

Grove Park Inn
290 Macon Avenue
Asheville, NC 28804
800-438-5800
groveparkinn.com

Joshua P. Warren's Asheville Tourism Center and Free Museum

asheviIletourcenter.com

Mystery Hill

129 Mystery Hill Lane
Blowing Rock, NC 28605
828-264-2792
exploreboone.com/things-to-do/attractions/mystery-hill

Old Settler's Cemetery

200 West 5th Street
Charlotte, NC 28202

Tweetsie Railroad

300 Tweetsie Railroad Lane
Blowing Rock, NC 28605
800-526-5740
tweetsie.com

FURTHER READING

LIST OF BOOKS USED IN RESEARCH

Auchincloss, Louis. *The Vanderbilt Era: Profiles of a Gilded Age.* Collier Books, 1990.

Barrett, John G. *The Civil War in North Carolina.* UNC Press, 1995.

Blackman, Ann. *Wild Rose: Rose O'Neale Greenhow, Civil War Spy.* Random House, 2006.

Bradley, Mark L. *Last Stand in the Carolinas: The Battle of Bentonville.* Da Capo Press, 1996.

Glatthaar, Joseph T. *The March to the Sea and Beyond: Sherman's Troops in the Savannah and Carolinas Campaigns, updated ed.* LSU Press, 1995.

Gould, William, IV. *Diary of a Contraband: The Civil War Passage of a Black Sailor.* Stanford University Press, 2002.

Gragg, Rod. *Confederate Goliath: The Battle of Fort Fisher, updated ed.* Harper Collins, 2006.

Hassler, William W. *The General to His Lady: The Civil War Letters of William Dorsey Pender to Fanny Pender.* UNC Press, 1965.

Hughes, Nathaniel Cheairs. *Bentonville: The Final Battle of Sherman and Johnston.* UNC Press, 1996.

Redford, Dorothy Spruill and D'Orso, Michael. *Somerset Homecoming: Recovering a Lost Heritage.* UNC Press, 2000.

Stiles, T. J. *The First Tycoon: The Epic Life of Cornelius Vanderbilt.* Vintage, 2010.

Terrell, Bob and Roberts, Ralph. *The Will Harris Murders: November 13, 1906, a Night in Which Asheville Was a Tougher Town Than Tombstone and Dodge City Rolled into One.* Land of the Sky Books, 2001.

Whedbee, Charles Harry. *The Flaming Ship of Ocracoke and Other Tales of the Outer Banks.* John F. Blair, 1971.

Whedbee, Charles Harry. *Outer Banks Mysteries & Seaside Stories.* John F. Blair, 1978.

ACKNOWLEDGMENTS

I must thank many people for this book. To begin, I have to thank the stars of this book, which are the ghosts themselves. Many of them were kind enough to show themselves to me while I visited their homes and gravesites, and I appreciate their time very much.

I was also surprised and amused that when I returned home from my travels and began writing this book, that one curious ghost came to visit me often as I would write. He wouldn't say much, preferring to stand quietly next to me while looking over my shoulder as I wrote each day. I would always sense his presence first by smelling tobacco smoke entering my office as I wrote. No one in our home smokes, nor do we allow anyone to smoke in our home, so it would catch me off guard at first as I would wonder where that smell was coming from. Now I've grown accustomed to it as he appears often when I write.

During his visits, he would stay for a good period of time, and he appeared to like what I was writing. I would be in deep concentration during these times, not wanting to lose my train of thought of what I wanted to say. One day my husband walked into my office as I had just finished writing for the day, and he squinted his eyes and began to wave his hand in front of his face and asked me, "Where is that smoke coming from?" He was looking all around my office, trying to find the source and then said, "It smells like tobacco smoke. Where in the world would this be coming from?"

He's a technical, scientific-minded man, and I remained quiet for a minute while he searched the entire room trying to discern where the smell was coming from. Exhausted by his efforts and finding nothing, he sat down to chat with me. I told him that a ghost had been coming to see me while I wrote the book and that I expected he would remain with me throughout the course of writing the book. I then explained that when he appears, the heavy scent of smoke is the first indication that he is here in spirit. My husband was not surprised by this news, as ghosts have visited me throughout my life and he's witnessed their visits in our home and during our travels.

Our little Chihuahua, Griffin, also senses ghosts and spirits when they appear, and we find him from time to time barking at a spirit that he has caught wind of as he attempts to tell them to move on. He's very protective and is our fierce, otherworldly guard dog. Chihuahuas have a history of being psychic and connected with the spiritual planes. The Toltecs of Mexico understood this well about the Chihuahua breed, also that the dog is a companion guide for the human soul. So I must also thank Griffin, my beloved white Chihuahua pup, for his constant companionship and guard-dog patrol during my ghost-hunting adventures.

A huge thank-you and enormous gratitude and appreciation go to my son, Brandon Ambrose, whose wit, wisdom, and generosity always entertain and inspire me. Brandon is an accomplished outdoor photographer who loves to travel. He was willing to take this journey with me to explore Ghost Hunting North Carolina, and his assistance was essential to my getting this book completed. All of the photographs in this book were taken by Brandon Ambrose, with the exceptions being the photos of the Star Hotel, which were provided to me by Gary Spivey, and the Page-Walker, Hillcrest Tree, and Grove Park photos, which I took.

I asked Brandon, after our adventures were done for the book, which place had been the most haunted to him, and his reply was Somerset Place Plantation. While there, he ventured out deep into the woods to have a look in the forest and experienced the presence of an entity following him through the woods that wasn't happy to have him around.

High on my list to thank is Tim, my partner in life and love. Without him, I would not be able to accomplish all that I am able to do. He's my rock, my love, and my soulmate. He's also one of the finest men that I have ever had the privilege to know.

A special thank-you also goes to Gary Spivey, who provided the photos of the Star Hotel, including the vortex around the fountain and gardens. The reports continue to come from people who experience overwhelmingly positive moments at the fountain as it offers them a view to the spirit realms.

I would also like to extend a tremendous amount of gratitude to my editor, John Kachuba. John and I met several years before *Ghost Hunting North Carolina* was conceived, and I've always enjoyed our talks. He's a special man with a talent for writing and editing, and his students are very lucky to have the opportunity to study with him. He's been a blessing in my life, and if you haven't checked out the books he's written for the America's Haunted Road Trip series, I suggest you do, for he covers several states in great haunting detail.

I would also like to thank everyone at Clerisy Press for all that they do and for the creation and delivery of this series. As I spoke with people during my travels and described the book to them, so many were delighted with the idea of such a wonderful way to teach history and to encourage families and friends to visit the rich variety of historic sites in each state, along with having the fun and sometimes fright of visiting haunted sites.

It goes without saying, as I try to say this as often as possible, I am most grateful to my family, my friends, my colleagues, and the fans of *Explore Your Spirit with Kala*. My friends, and you know who you are, I appreciate you being there for me and going for the occasional ride with me somewhere for a little adventure and fun. To my fans of the *Explore Your Spirit with Kala Show,* I appreciate your support so dearly. The emails I receive from you, the Facebook and Twitter posts, all inspire me to do more and deliver more to you every day. Thanks for taking the ride with me, and I hope you'll do just that now; pile in the car with some friends and let's go *Ghost Hunting North Carolina*.

In love, gratitude, and joy,
—Kala

ABOUT the AUTHOR

Kala Ambrose is an award-winning author, renowned intuitive, wisdom teacher, intuitive interior decorator, podcaster, and lifestyle coach. Known as **Your Travel Guide to the Other Side®**, Kala helps entrepreneurs, wisdom seekers, and visionaries live their best lives.

Author of six books, including *Spirits of New Orleans, Ghost Hunting North Carolina, The Awakened Aura, The Awakened Psychic, 9 Life Altering Lessons,* and *The Awakened Dreamer,* Kala is considered one of the country's foremost experts on mystic spirituality and psychic/intuitive ability. Her work with the understanding of aura, energy fields, and color has brought her three major awards for her book, *The Awakened Aura,* which has been printed in six languages.

An interactive teacher on a mission to educate, entertain, and inspire, she's a motivational speaker; highly sought after wisdom teacher, presenter, and coach; and has lectured and taught at numerous centers and conferences, including the Omega Institute, Edgar Cayce's ARE, Lily Dale Assembly, John Edward's Infinite Quest, the Learning Annex, and many more.

Whether she's discussing life-enhancing topics on her podcast, *The Explore Your Spirit with Kala Show,* writing about metaphysical topics, reporting on new discoveries in the scientific and spiritual arenas, or teaching groups around the country, fans around the world tune in daily for Kala's inspirational musings and lively thought-provoking conversations. Find her at ExploreYourSpirit.com